# Durable Balance

# Durable Balance

Creating Legacies in
Neighborhood Charities

**Tom Sims**

**Durable Balance: Creating Legacies in Neighborhood Charities**

Copyright © 2020 Tom Sims

Books may be ordered at www.durablebalancebook.com.

The views expressed in this work are solely those of the author and do not necessarily reflect the views of the publisher, and the publisher hereby disclaims any responsibility for them.

ISBN: 978-1-79489-237-8

To My Wife, Jacquie

# CONTENTS

## INTRODUCTION

What comes easy doesn't last, and what lasts doesn't come easy. This book is for the person responsible for raising funds at a neighborhood nonprofit, whether you're paid or not. It guides you through the process of meeting the immediate needs of your nonprofit as well as planning for its long-term survival while building trust with donors. And that's all together and all at once. It's not impossible. It's not easy either.

Over the years, I've experienced personal and professional growth, and it usually came hand-in-hand with extreme disappointment. At one place, the director wanted to bring in a consultant friend, and I was out the door despite my best efforts. My time at that same place gave me a solid understanding of the local philanthropic landscape, an education I carried to other jobs well into the future. But it was tough being let go, one of the few times that ever happened to me. Still, I was able to learn and grow.

After the trial comes a fork in the road. On one path, there is learning and rising up from the ashes. On the other, there is self-pity with silver linings undetected.

It's time to choose.

When it comes to raising money for charity, everyone starts out with passion and diligence. The road can get tough. The road *will* get tough. At each crossroad, there is the chance to think only of paying bills for the current year and let tomorrow take care of itself.

But there is another course.

As fundraisers, we talk to contributors about leaving a legacy, but that is not on the shoulders of donors alone. It's on us fundraisers as well. It is at the heart of servant leadership, and as challenging as it is, it is the best course of action. It is an estate of good will we all hope to pass along in the ministries we serve.

How many times have you heard it said, "Don't leave money on the table?" It's less about what you're leaving on the table and more about what you're leaving behind at your charity.

# PART I

## *Charity Begins*

*"People will forget what you said, people will forget what you did, but people will never forget how you made them feel."*

Maya Angelou

For more than thirty years, I have (like most people) been asked, "What do you do for a living?" My answer, "fundraising," causes mixed reactions. One person said, "Aww, isn't that sweet? You help people." Yes, it sounded as patronizing as that. Another person actually rummaged through his wallet and pulled out ten crumpled up dollar bills. "Here," he said giving them to me, "give this to your cause." True story. However, my favorite reaction was while talking with a neighbor. He was hard of hearing, and English wasn't his native language. I told him I was a fundraiser. His response was, "Oh, so you are a professional beggar, yes?" I replied, "It's more like being a salesperson to bring out the good in all of us." Maybe he didn't understand or maybe he couldn't hear me, but he smiled. You may never know how people will react to your words, but you can always strive to impress them with your compassion, listening skills, empathy, and savvy. They'll never forget the way you made them feel.

# CHAPTER 1

## *Closer than Home*

Charity may begin at home, but where it goes depends on every one of us. All of us donors, volunteers, board leaders, CEOs, fundraisers, neighbors, even every beneficiary.

All of us.

Charity really begins much closer than home. It begins in your heart, in your mind, in your spirit. It begins at the essential core of your being. Do you care about others or do you care only about yourself? That's the spot, that's where charity begins. It extends to your family, that home we talk about. But can it extend further than that? For many it can and thankfully it has.

Charities start with people who want to help, and I've seen this at soup kitchens, animal shelters, arts groups, historic restoration projects, churches, and many other nonprofits. People want to help because they care about others in need. I've witnessed that care in the volunteers who gave their time, hundreds of donations that came through the mail or online in just one day, foundations that awarded grants, and families who made exceptional gifts. My teams have solicited those gifts, scheduled those volunteers, and had coffee with the people who could offer amazing donations. Our work in preparing letter campaigns, writing grant applications, and hosting fundraising events are all done with the best intentions. The various teams I've managed have raised more than $35 million over the years. Some members on those teams have been the finest people I know.

All of that caring leads nonprofits to grow its programs and impact, and there is a need for much more than charity alone. They need warehouses and computer systems, vehicles and postage stamps. They need to hire more people to get the program work done. Many of the leaders at these nonprofits are encouraging and driven with charity at the center of their hearts. However, other executives come under fire mostly for mismanagement of one sort or another. Much of this is usually driven by ego, greed, incompetence, or a mix of all—and I've seen it all. This bad conduct is one of the many reasons overall charitable giving is down. According to a recent surveys, giving to some charitable organizations may be up but for many giving is mostly flat or in decline.

Lower revenue is only one problem facing nonprofit development offices. The other is staff turnover, which presents a major hindrance with the average professional lasting only 18 months in one position, according to most benchmark indicators. This presents a real crisis for charities. We are not going to focus on turnover necessarily, but rather one of its worst byproducts: lack of long-term planning. When these fundraisers are here today and gone less than two years later, will they have time to plan for future funding? More than likely, they will only have time to work hard in making budget goals in the only full year they're at the organization.

Many nonprofits don't have a rainy day fund or they struggle to keep any money in it. Endowment plans (or accounts, if a nonprofit was ever able to start one) seem stalled. Many organization seem enslaved by their annual fund, setting the counter back to zero at the beginning of every fiscal year only to start the fundraising hunt anew all over again. It's exhausting.

Let's talk about planning for what I call a durable balance.

Durable balance is a harmonious system among three separate fund buckets that provide long-term stability for a charity. Fundraisers should work to fill these buckets knowing their goals and how they are built both separately and in consideration of one another. Balancing these three is key to any nonprofit's long-term success. The buckets are: annual (or every day); reserve (or rainy day); and endowment (or forever).

*Annual or "every day" funds.* Every year, charities get donations by sending mailers, hosting parties, and asking foundations and companies for grants. In that same year, they deplete most of that money with ongoing expenses, and then they hope there isn't a deficit. This is the one account we tend to focus on the most. We want to build it up every year so we can do more to advance our mission.

*Reserve or "rainy day" funds.* This fund can also be grown each year (preferably with larger gifts or a surplus from last year's annual fund) and should be used discerningly for unexpected costs, but we hope it can be preserved for the future. In lean years (that "rainy day"), organizations use this money with promises to build it back up. But rainy years are called that for a reason, and it's difficult to get money back to that account.

*Endowment or "forever" funds.* The nonprofit uses only the interest of the fund, preserving the principal for use in perpetuity. Smaller nonprofits may say, "Leave the endowments to Harvard, we're not Harvard." I know they say it because I was one of those fundraisers who said it. And there may be some validity to that position, but you may miss something big …in fact, very big.

For reasons already outlined, fewer donations and increasing staff turnover, development offices find it difficult to rise above the fray in raising more funds than is needed in a given year. So what happens when there's an unexpected transformative gift (yes, it still happens once in a while)? If you've been in development long enough, you've experienced it.

The windfall may be that six or seven figure check either a bequest or in memory of someone. It comes in, and you start your happy dancing. Your leadership starts dancing too. Board, CEO, CFO, everybody is dancing.

Once you're all done dancing, now what are you going to do? Well, the CFO is saying, "Let's get that check right into the bank!" The CEO says, "Let me tell the Board we got a transformative gift!" You're saving, "What a relief! We might make budget this year, and I've just been given another year at this place!"

But what will your Board say?

More importantly what will your Board Treasurer say? With any luck, she'll say she wants this gift to be set aside and *not* counted as annual operating funds. Oh, you may not see that as "luck," right? Is that treasurer going to rob you of your good fortune? Right after you're all done with the high fives and dancing, is there going to be rain on the parade?

We get in such "need it now, you never know what the future can bring" mode that we sometimes can't stop to think of how a substantial gift can help long term.

And it's not just the development office. Boards and executives also can get caught in the trap of satisfying the needs of the annual fund and letting the next generation of leaders think of what to do for a rainy day. These very same leaders give a new fundraiser nine months to get up to speed and then want a "fresh perspective" after a year and let them go (thus contributing to that high turnover).

The answer to all of the struggles may start in embracing the durable balance. Building and maintaining an enduring equilibrium among the three funds is the key to short term gains and long-term stability.

Before you begin to talk about a major gift program, or capital campaign, or especially the next budget cycle for your annual fund – you need to talk about a durable balance. Would you know what to do with a six-figure gift if you received one? I mean after high fives and dancing. Some teams have an idea, others do not.

Consider the following:

*Surplus year over year:* if your annual fund is constantly struggling to end the year with a surplus, there is significant work that needs to be done in that area. You may have to slay some sacred programming or consider staff restructuring, but you need to cut costs somewhere.

*Mapping revenue and expenses:* First, exhaust planning for your revenue sources. Special events, mailings, digital outreach – it all needs to be completely mapped out. Realistically forecast what revenue you can bring in. Next, forecast your expenses. If expenses are too high, guess what area needs work? Hint: it's not revenue.

*We are not magicians, we're fundraisers!* The development department is not Santa Claus! Nobody gets a wish list to ask for whatever shortfall gap needs to be filled mid-year. When you map revenue correctly, then there is a scientific way in which you will earn money over the next year. There is no special formula that comes along mid-year to save the day. This is not to say you don't tweak or refine plans to optimize your returns, but you cannot rely on those adjustments.

*Build a plan for surplus:* Once you see a surplus, you can build a plan for what do with it. The plan could be simple but know what you're going to do with it. Have a portion of it set aside to start a new reserve account. Or perhaps there will be a portion that will actually start an endowment.

*Some ideas fly, others walk:* New ideas to create revenue need to be mapped out to measure if there is a realistic return on investment. Each philanthropic idea has an expense side too. If there is good ROI, let it fly. New program ideas which only incur expenses without revenue need much more time to be mapped out (maybe until the next fiscal year).

*Major gift solicitation planning:* This goes beyond the annual fundraising plan, which is driven by direct mail, special events, and grants. A major gifts program needs to start with a plan. Maybe map how you'll split those five- and six-figure gifts among the annual, reserve, and endowment accounts in a set percentage. Then stick to the plan. The better part of this book is dedicated to major gift solicitation; because of all the ways you can make money, major gifts is one of the only ones that can transform your charity's future. The other reason this is such an important pursuit is that mainly it frustratingly happens in fits and starts for many nonprofits.

*Reserve funds*: Annual funds are used every day, and endowments are a heavily regulated account that cannot be spent down. Reserve funds are in between and shouldn't be treated like either of the other two. Allow for one year of losses of reserves but not two. If the board needs to approve policies on this, so be it. It's better to have something in writing as a guide.

Someone has bestowed a transformative gift, maybe even the biggest one you've ever received. Most places will throw that into expenses for that year, and all that money is gone (it probably was before it was received). Some organizations that take those gifts and put them in an endowment, and none but the interest may ever be spent. Imagine an alternative. Imagine telling that very generous donor that you used their gift a little for today but you've established a portion of that gift for continued giving. You tell them it's in a fund where the interest every year pays for a scholarship, or fresh food for a pantry, or some other recurring expense each year—and the money will do so for generations to come. Tell them their great grandchildren will be able to see the good works that continue through their single gift made "way back when." What will happen when you go back to that donor a couple years from now and ask for another major gift? Think they might be a little more open to repeat their performance of astounding generosity?

A durable balance is just that. It is nonprofit finances in a balancing act that meets every year's expenses with the stability of knowing money will be there for the future. Starting with a strong annual fund helps grow your other two funds and keeps them strong in perpetuity. It takes planning and wise counsel, but it can be achieved. And as you look back on your own professional ministry, you'll see that you didn't simply "get by," you grew something that will continue years after you've retired.

## CHAPTER 2

## *Confessions of a Professional Beggar*

There is nothing wrong with a career in fundraising, except that it can be hand-to-mouth, exhausting, and in a perpetual state of uncertainty. Appealing, right? One of my first jobs out of college was at a professional association of hospital laboratory managers. My job was to get sponsors to help pay for our annual conference. Wait that was actually the job I grew into. I started there working on the newsletter, and eventually started creating marketing materials for its annual conference. Eventually, I was soliciting big companies for sponsorship.

My first major grant was from a multi-national diagnostic machine company (you'd know the name right away). How it came about was interesting. An article came out in the *New England Journal of Medicine* that argued hospital laboratories were drawing too much blood samples. Those are fightin' words to my constituents (you, know, lab manages who draw blood from patients at hospitals). I showed the article to my CEO and said, "Let's survey our members about how they draw only enough blood and no more. The manufacturer of a new diagnostic machine that boasts about using smaller blood samples would love the exposure."

The money came in, and it was exhilarating to know my idea made it happen! I knew I'd always want to be on the fundraising side of this business. The rainmaker. After I was done high fiving myself when that money came in, I handed that project off to the research team and got out there and get more money. Such is the lifecycle of nonprofit revenue. It comes in, gets used, and new money is needed.

Can you imagine a job where at the beginning of each new fiscal year, you need to start the revenue clock all over again? New fiscal year, new urgency to create the fund pool you created last year. Well, of course we can imagine it. In nearly every for-profit business, every year (maybe every month) new customers need to be cultivated and creative ways to retain the old ones need to be found. Otherwise the company doesn't make it. It's called sales and marketing. It's the oldest profession in the book.

Have you ever really thought about how you're a salesperson and not a fundraiser? If you have, you've probably been at this a long time. Either way, maybe the words "hand-to-mouth, exhausting, and in a perpetual state of uncertainty" ring true.

Hand-to-mouth is a term that needs no explanation. And sure there's "never a dull moment" and yes there may be "no rest for the weary," two phrases actually used quite a bit in the fundraising office. But burn out happens. This may be a major contributor to the 18-month turnover experienced among fundraising professionals.

The state of uncertainty is real. You can never really say from one year to the next whether you're going to meet your goal. The cause is doing wonderful work, but are competing groups stepping into your space? The number of nonprofits created each year is staggering. It seems that someone finds a "supposedly unfulfilled" need left by other nonprofits, and they try to fill that niche. They attract some of your donors, and you're struggling to now fill the gap in your own budget. The number of charities that close each year is equally staggering.

So you're in sales. Fundraising sales. Marketing to other's good will. And do you want to finish the year strong? "Year," you say, "how about finishing the quarter strong." Now that's the sales mentality! Embrace it! Let's face it, it's better than being called a professional beggar!

Business doesn't begin until sales calls are made. You've seen the factory. The floor workers park in Lot C. As they walk past Lot A, where all the sales people park their much fancier cars, they look on in envy. Maybe that resentment is justified. The sales team may be a real bunch of jerks. They might be loud. They may be unruly. And they may even look down on the floor workers.

But if they are any good, they bring in the business. They get perks if they're numbers are on target. Sometimes that's a moving target. In nonprofit land, the target is almost always moving up, spiking if leadership anticipates a shortfall.

You're on the sales team. And for many small nonprofits, you alone are the sales team. If that's the case, find volunteers who can act as your development committee and soon you'll be in good company. I was working for one nonprofit, and apart from a two gift processing staff on my team, primarily it was my job to get results. And I was in a remote office across the hall from my two staff members. And I was pretty much left alone. This gave me free reign, and while I may not have fully appreciated it at the time, it was one of the best experiences of my life.

I spent my days establishing messaging and collateral, making a plan to follow up with donors who could make more significant gifts, and honing my direct mail skills. One area where they needed help was special events, and I needed help organizing them. I started building a team of volunteers that acted as an event committee. They were a dedicated bunch, and every time they came to a meeting I made sure I had snacks and drinks. If you've got a committee and not particularly active, start hosting meetings and put out a little food—oh and bring on new members. That'll freshen things up a little. You need the sales support to get your job done.

What does a good sales team do? It canvasses for sales and leads, right? This is what your direct mail program should be doing for you. Everyone should understand what a direct mail campaign is, even if you haven't worked on one you certainly have received such mail. There is a whole art and science to it. How many mailings does your nonprofit send each year? You usually know if it's too much. Or you don't mail much because you don't want your donors to complain there is too much solicitation. Can you squeeze just one more in next year? Maybe you say you do just enough and you've got a sophisticated system. Wonderful, what are you doing with the data being generated? Are you culling it to find those donors who are showing they really enjoy supporting your work so you can solicit for a legacy gift?

The fact is: sales is sales. Whether you're trying to sell cars, homes, Tupperware, or a good cause, you're in sales. You've got to start thinking in terms of forecasts, trends, and "roll up your sleeves" solicitation. When I first started my career, it was like sales was a dirty word. The sales jobs all seemed skeevy, like sleazy, for schmoozers who either were duds without enough charm to sell gloves in Alaska or alternatively someone so slick the Alaskan would rather let their hands freeze.

Want to see the worst of the worst in sales from the movies. Google the line "Put that coffee down" and the iconic scene appears from *Glengarry Glen Ross* from 1992. It's a downer of a film about bottom feeder sales people. In this scene, Alec Baldwin plays a top sales person who comes to the office one night to deliver a "motivational talk" to underperforming sales staff. It's an ugly presentation, but it's fun to watch. This should never be what nonprofit sales is like (or any sales job).

My motivation speech would be different. Using the most effective resources you can afford, you do your best and hope for the same. Throughout your whole career, wherever you are, you're not working. You're selling. Yes, you're selling your own brand of work and you're promoting charity. You've got one chance to make an impact at one point in time for your cause, one chance to do something uniquely you and amazingly impressive because of you.

The good news is the coffee isn't only for closers and you don't have to be such a high octane sales person all the time. But to the extent you're selling you are succeeding. We're all in sales. Yes, fundraiser or not, each one of us spends our time selling our opinion, our accomplishments, or our agenda. Maybe you're selling a reason for a raise, or your selling yourself to a new company for a better job. We sell our points of view, our takes, our stands. We sell the reason for our existence.

Most times, people want to sell you the reason why they're so important at what they do. It answers the fundamental question, "Do I matter?" The fact is: you do matter, for as long as you are around. For as long as you put the spin on those plates in the air, they're spinning for the reasons that matter most to you. Once you stop spinning, someone else will invariably drop some plates, continue some others, and put their own plates in the air. Then they'll matter at that time, and you'll be in another place spinning other plates as somebody else's replacement.

After five years at one charity, it was time to move on. That wasn't because my work was necessarily finished, but it was because my new structure was built. This was a platform this charity had never seen before, one that could optimize how we managed grants, reached out to new donors via direct mail, and ensured we captured every peer-to-peer and online gift possible. We had established an event calendar that was as strategic as it was full. We knew how many large galas we could run, how many third-party events we could take on as a beneficiary, and how many smaller benefits we could manage. In five years, my remarkable team led double-digit growth, and my one director was ready to take my job. I found another opportunity, left, and she indeed got that job. Good managers work themselves out of a job, right? You're so good at managing the work of others, providing them such outstanding direction, that they can end up doing your job. Why would you fight that? There are other jobs. Let them shine.

Think of another movie: *About Schmidt*, a 2002 comedy drama starring Jack Nicholson. In it, Jack is older and retires from his job. He leaves his successor boxes and boxes filled with papers and folders with the understanding that this was his legacy and leaving the new worker with a place to pick up where Jack left off. The following week, he visits the office to see how things are going, and all of those boxes are outside of a full dumpster waiting to get picked up.

Your time will come, and then your time will go. The papers you leave behind will be tossed, and somebody else will start fresh. But they can't throw away the events you grew, they can't toss the relationships you've nurtured with important donors. In one arts festival where I worked for many years, the summer camp for kids and the flagship festival program were fully operational. Unfortunately, everything was facing certain collapse under the unbelievable weight of a heavy deficit. In a few years, I was able to cut spending and grow donations. I created lasting relationships with people I will likely remain friends with for life. Together, we eliminated the deficit, built a surplus, and the show went on for more than a decade later.

This is your moment in time to make a difference. What change can you make? What fortunes can you turn around? What structure can you build that will endure? Spend the time to make the three funds fully operational and lasting long after you're gone. Make your plans, institute your programs, and shake the hands of anyone willing to help.

Go sell it!

# CHAPTER 3
## *Make Budget, Not Magic*

It was one of my most rewarding jobs, fundraising to help families who needed food. Imagine a place where every dollar raised provided another meal to a child, senior, or family in need. Guess when we had our busiest time of year? Staff would say, "It's the holiday season, bring that fourth quarter magic." They were talking about an avalanche of donations that started at Thanksgiving and kept going right up until midnight, December 31. This was before tax code changes essentially made it less attractive to itemize deductions for smaller gifts. Like the letters to Santa poured on the judge's desk in the movie *Miracle on 34th Street*, those donations did flow in and the generosity of our donors did seem magical. We provided food to families in need, so of course donors wanted to especially help around the holidays.

But was it all magic? We had big plans for that fourth quarter. We did not just sit back and leave it up to the goodness in people's hearts. If there was ever a time nonprofits mail to their donors for money, anyone with a mailbox knows this time of year brings on the most mail they ever saw. For us, we planned one touchpoint after another—mail, emails, social media, and other ways to reach out to our donors to ensure we were top of mind when it came to that "magical" quarter. There were even phone calls to donors who we knew had the ability to be very generous, no hard sell but rather a voicemail to say, "Please let us know if you want any ideas for special gifting opportunities at this time of year."

I would explain to staff how the magic was planned more than a year in advance, so everything was very well orchestrated. That's not to say my job wasn't like that of a magician. They wave a wand, set off some flash of light, and "presto" magic happens. The audience could only see what was happening on the surface, and it was my job to make sure that they didn't see all the work that went behind it.

Still, to call it magic was irksome.

What happens sometimes was even worse. Not only can a boss call that time of year mystical, but there was a hope that I could increase the wizardry as needed. On demand. As in, "Are we in a pickle! What can you do to raise $200,000 for a shortfall we're likely to experience?"

The fact is, I was constantly tweaking our plan to look for ways to find more money. Sometimes it would work, but if expenses were not kept in check what did it matter? Eventually, I came to a place where I had a plan, and I had contingency plans as I made note of what was working and what wasn't. Did that mailer to every house in a certain high wealth zip code bring in healthy returns? Let's do another one. Things like that.

I never consider these a "plan B." In life, there is no plan B. Don't you love when celebrities in whatever walk of life be it entertainment, sports, or business talk about not having a plan B? "I made it, and you can too, but you have to give up on a plan B." That's what they will say. Yet invariably you hear about how these people work some placeholder job until they "made it." What of those celebrities that rise to success only to come to a terrible, or worse tragic, ending? Was that plan B?

The fact is: you should not have a plan B. All of what you're doing is plan A. Every side road you take is part of plan A. Certainly, you want to be focused. Absolutely, you don't want to be ruled by distraction. But life can throw you curveballs, reality can leave you scrambling. Consider those diversions as far ahead in advance as you can, but they all can lead you to a better place in your big plan. You know the one. Plan A. The only plan you've got. Consider all the variations to your plan. Make sure you know where you can purposely make a left or a right away from the center to eventually reach goal. In your plan A, remember the roadblocks. They don't lead you to drop back to your plan B, they only help you revise your plan A.

Eventually, I had to tell the entire staff helping to feed all those families, "This fundraising department is not Santa Claus! You can't wish it and hope we can make it come true. We have a plan. That plan has contingencies to possibly do more. But we made a budget, and we're sticking to it. If you're overspending, I have one piece of advice: stop overspending. Rein in your costs!"

I'm paraphrasing from memory, but it was something like that—exclamation points and all.

It was a pivotal moment in my career. I was finally telling myself and everyone else that we need to be deliberate, and we need to have a plan. When revenue is down, you can pull out those contingencies to see if you can turn the tide. Those contingency parts of Plan A should be at the ready, but cutting costs is the primary way to respond to a forecast shortfall in revenue.

As we begin to approach the subject of the three revenue buckets, it will be important to understand how planning helps get us to goal. Without a plan, you're simply stashing what could be perpetuating funds to be used up like so much "paper in fire."

And if you don't have a plan, all of your fundraising is about the hand-to-mouth. Is that what you want? I don't know a fundraiser who doesn't think about how they can leave an impact for their cause well into the future. They talk about it. They may even set out to plan for it. But then it all goes up, like paper in fire.

And don't look for help from your leadership, your CEO or CFO, or the board of trustees even, they're looking at this kind of planning from you. We are the fundraisers and the leaders of that discipline, and we are the best hope for the cause.

There was this one nonprofit where we had a significant gift that came in. Six digits like we have never seen before! Everybody was elated. But there wasn't a plan. That gift was put right into the annual fund and used up. We didn't see it coming, and we barely got to see it go. Actual expenses rose above budget and far outweighed budgeted revenue. Budgeted revenue, as in "that's all I said we can conceivably make." So it went up. It could've made for a great perpetual gift, but it was gone.

Proper planning gives you the insights and structure to make sure that every gift realized (especially the significant ones) are truly transformative. You owe that to your cause, you owe that to your own career.

Make the decision to be purposeful about your plan.

# PART II

## *The Three Funds*

*"Don't tell me where your priorities are. Show me where*
*you spend your money, and I'll tell you what they are."*

James W. Frick

There are three funds for any nonprofit, and they all require a lot of work. Don't neglect one to keep the others out of the red. They all represent something very different to the charity you work so hard to maintain. You can have a plan for all three and watch them grow. Alternatively, you can keep saying that "endowments are for much bigger charities" and keep the exhausting cycle of building your operating fund year after year. What do these funds enable you to do, and how can you approach them all with a sense of purpose and drive?

# CHAPTER 4
## *Annual/Everyday Fund*

Of the three funds discussed in this book, the first one is the most recognizable and easiest to understand. The annual fund, what we call the everyday or operating fund, is the fund you budget for every year. It's the one that keeps your operations running every day. It may be the one that keeps you up at night.

How you deposit to this fund varies by organization. For some, it's a steady diet of direct mail, fundraising events, and pretty much any other source of revenue we can find. If you're not sure what direct mail is, check your mailbox this week. You know something will come in from a charity you've either given to in the past or one that is targeting you. It's the one that is helping others and needs your support. And it's big business. Partnerships with local business, online donation tools, and of course today peer-to-peer or social media fundraising. This is the online fundraising with which everybody has reason to be enamored.

But let's start with the Holy Grail of the annual fund solicitation design: direct mail. Who doesn't love direct mail? Oh, I can tell you. The maybe 2% of the population who registers their complaint with you, and sometimes over and over again, to tell you to stop mailing stuff to them!

Yes, there are those people. Then there's a big chunk of people, the clear majority of people. This population accounts for 90% of your direct mail audience. Who are they? The ones who simply throw away the mail pieces you send.

Direct mail gets a bad reputation for reasons that may see obvious but are not necessarily true. It's a waste of the nonprofit's money. I heard this a lot. But when you target your mailing list, get better responses from donors with gifts that are higher as well, you see that it more than pays for itself. For some causes, if I could've hovered by helicopter over high wealth zip codes and dropped millions of pieces on the unsuspecting homes below, I would have. Blanketing an entire high wealth zip code is in some cases the best way to get new donors to support your cause.

Some of the fundraisers reading this may be saying out loud, "But what about social media?" To which I say, "direct mail is still dominates when it comes to getting the word out." I've developed direct mail programs on my own – and I have developed them with professional consultants. Either way, I have been the cause for the pain of many a neighbor who goes to the mailbox to find one (or more) of my letters in it.

Throughout the years, it's always been important to seek the best direct mail approach. Try to be intelligent about it. Try to know who your donors are, right? The ones that haven't given in 36 months, send them a smaller piece. Know the ones you gave recently, maybe send them every piece every month. Unless of course that donor responds every month, then why wouldn't you send fewer mailers to them? Professional beggar, maybe, but I'm trying not to be annoying about it.

With just a little tweaking to an algorithm, nonprofits can be a little less annoying. Yes, it's complicated. But ultimately it pays off with fewer calls asking to stop sending mail. It pays off in not only more donations but higher donations. I've seen it happen. Take the time to build an annual fund more deliberately, more mindfully. It's called market segmentation. In other words, know your donors maybe not to the most extreme detail but in some detail.

Ultimately, segmenting the market is the smartest approach to take for the future of a nonprofit organization. It will help you target more significant donors with less overwhelming campaigns. In fact, it will help you target them with more personal, high touch outreach.

What else do you do to make an annual fund goals? Host a gala? Or some other fundraising event? How does that work for most nonprofits? It's better to choose fewer events and build equity in each of them rather than have too many events that people get desensitized to invitations to join the next one.

In some cases, building equity in fewer events is a sound strategy. Three solid events in any given year could really help create one-third to a half of your budget. But consider the cost. Oh, you say you already have counted the exact cost? Have you calculated the most important cost? Volunteer power expended is the highest cost of any fundraising event calendar. Think about it. The more events you have, the less inclined people are to show up to help out. Everybody is busy. Or maybe your volunteer base is getting older. Or maybe they're just getting fatigued. Either way, you will find as your charity gets more mature, it will be more difficult to engage volunteers to a higher level of service. Factor it in.

Introduce new events slowly. Enter into them with a lot of forethought. What time of year is best to host the event? How intense is the volunteer activity? And of course how much will cost in space rental, volunteer power, or whatever? And it's not like once you have your event calendar that it is locked in. Quite the contrary. It is constantly fluid and moving. Something works one year that doesn't work the next year or two years down the road. It's better to say, "We try to do three events a year – no matter what they are. And they must make a certain amount of money for us to keep doing them."

And do all events need to be big money makers? That all depends. Ah, you thought I was going to say, "Absolutely!" Well it really does depend. An event can be a simple opportunity to have potential donors get together to engage them. Not every time does the money need to come out. Later down the road, when you send that direct mail piece, you may get a better result if you got people together at a no pressure social.

And what about online, peer-to-peer marketing. This is more than just an email broadcast that solicits a gift through a website donation page. This is where people are going to their social media account and engage their friends to help give as well. If you are not an international organization with millions of online subscribers and followers, you may find this to be a little less fruitful. That's not to say you shouldn't do it. It's important to be on all sorts of platforms, but be mindful when treading into these waters.

We all know about our annual fund. We work it every day. It's what you wake up thinking about, sometimes way too early in the morning. It's what you jot notes to yourself about before going to bed so you don't stay awake all night thinking about it. It's with you every day like a friend (okay, maybe you don't see it as a friend, but don't get hostile!). Every nonprofit needs to get this one under control first. Without balance here, triple balance is not possible.

# CHAPTER 5

## *Reserve/Rainy Day Fund*

What is a reserve fund? At its most basic level it is an account that you don't touch unless absolutely necessary. This makes a lot of presumptions. First, let's assume a nonprofit is managed at an optimal level so that a surplus of funding is made available every year. Not only does that mean the reserve account doesn't get tapped, it also means that it's possible to add to that account with the surplus funding every year. That's a mighty big assumption. Maybe the best you can hope for is that you dip into the account during lean months and repay when the donations are flooding later in the year. Next assumption: that any catastrophic losses are covered some other way (insurance mostly).

In 30 plus years, I've managed at a lot of nonprofits. There were very few that had a robust reserve fund. The Nonprofit Finance Fund, which regularly studies the financial practices of the nonprofit sector, has surveyed nonprofits for several consecutive years to find that most nonprofits have only a month or two of cash in their reserves. A precarious spot indeed. And on the other hand, you can't have too much sitting in reserves. I had the privilege to say this only a few times in my career. "If you save more than year and a half worth in reserves long enough," I was told, "and the IRS may look at you funny."

How many nonprofits keep those reserves in a checking account? Some move those funds to CDs or other investments accounts. Above the year and a half or so the IRS will allow you to keep in reserves, and anything over that may begin a scholarship fund, a public awareness campaign, or a new service program.—or it could start an endowment. Starting that fund allows you to take dividends hopefully in perpetuity (or as long as you can manage it) for purposes of a charitable gesture in the community. If you've been wise stewards of your resources, you should have that reserve built up. Let's raise a glass to your success and for understanding the importance of good stewardship.

Like I said, it's a good problem to have, but without proper management it can become a real problem later. We have seen the biblical cautionary tale… store up grain in the good years in case you have lean years ahead. One nonprofit in my portfolio during my consulting years stored up some serious reserves in certificates of deposit. Not bad, but not exactly a high yield investment. Within a few years they were having to cash those CDs to help an ongoing operating deficit. They finally heeded my warnings about what was creating the deficit so they could resolve the shortfalls, but more about that in a later chapter.

Building a rainy day fund takes a whole lot of discipline from across the board. And by "board" I do mean "Board of Directors" and everybody else. Your CEO, you, your staff… everyone needs to be in the mix. Because the best way to build that fund is by having years in a surplus budget. And there is only one way to do that: sound management day in and day out.

Once you get into the habit of building that rainy day budget, you'll be excited by the results. Now you have to exercise the discipline not to use it for everyday needs. Like that leaky roof. Incorporate those kinds of normal challenges into your annual fund. Be skeptical of anyone (board member, finance team, volunteer) who keeps saying, "Hey what about all that money in our rainy day fund? Our roof leaks on rainy days? How about we use that money."

But what of that leaky roof? Should you host a special fundraiser to help pay for it? Isn't that what every nonprofit does who has to manage facilities like that? Maybe some, but not everyone. Think about how we host capital fundraisers? We try to go to some of our more affluent donors and get the thermometer 70% to goal, right? Then you go to the rank and file donor and tell them, "We're almost there. Let's get to goal!" Maybe the whole campaign is a success!

What happens next year when your floor begins to buckle or your windows need replacing... or your parking lot needs repaving. How many fundraisers have heard from a donor, "Didn't we just make a five-digit gift a year or so ago? You need more?"

If fundraisers shouldn't do a capital campaign or dip into the rainy day fund, what should be done? Here's where you need to get creative. Patch the roof for now and roll up your sleeves. Maybe you can find money from another place in the budget to cover some of the costs. Maybe you can get help on the roof as part of a solar power project. Sure, dip into the rainy day fund, but only minimally. I've seen alternatives work.

Getting imaginative in fundraising is an everyday occurrence, right? Creativity is woven into the fabric of stewardship. When you can demonstrate to a donor that you took extreme measures to make sure their money was spent wisely, you endear them and may get more funding as a result.

Donors are like every other part of your team, they want to be with the winners. If you find yourself in deficit spending year after year, you'll find your support is precarious no matter what your cause. I was meeting with a charity that spoke about how well they do year-over-year in maintaining a surplus budget. "We can't always point to deficit spending as a need for donor support," the director said. I stopped him on the spot.

Deficit spending is one of the worst selling points when trying to solicit funds. That you meet your needs each year is actually a plus. We can sell another reason for wanting a rainy day or forever fund. Frankly, without annual surplus budgets, anybody would be concerned about donating even a little to the cause let alone a significant gift.

Your rainy day fund should be sacred. It should even have board-approved policies for deposits as well as disbursements. Maybe a percentage every year that can go in or come out. Maybe a rolling percentage if you're good with it for many years in a row. There should be some formula for how you're going to protect and grow this fund.

If you can hold off raiding the rainy day fund successfully, you will soon find yourself in an even better position... being able to fund something that looks like a forever fund.

## CHAPTER 6
### *Endowment/Forever Fund*

The first time I was responsible for an endowment fund, it was for a small social service agency that did good work in forgotten, underserved communities. Before I joined them, they received a substantial gift that the donor wanted to be used as seed money for an endowment. By the time I started, the endowment had only a little more than when it started. And it didn't take me too long to figure out why. Endowments are like bank accounts except you can't touch any of the money; you can only use the interest that's generated from the account and at that you only had access to that money once a year. Every time a gift was made to that endowment, staff would groan and say, "You know we can't use anything but the interest on that money!" And at the time, I agreed. Because I was so focused on meeting annual operating revenue goals, I resisted soliciting gifts for that account. I thought, why would I want money I'm working hard to solicit ending up in an account that meant very little to what the nonprofit was doing day after day?

At this nonprofit, I learned the fundamental elements of an endowment. As referenced, it's like a bank account you can only use once a year and you can only withdraw the interest from the previous year. Let's say the interest is somewhere between two to seven percent. Think about that in terms of actual money going to an organization. If you have $100,000 in the account, interest would be about (say, at four percent) $4,000 every year. The good news, you'll have that $4,000 to use year after year after year. In 25 years, that equals $100,000—and your original $100,000 is still in the "bank" so that $4,000 will continue to pay out. And with any luck the account will grow as well. However, with a staff turnover rate of 18 months, who is thinking about what's going to happen 25 years from now? Besides, it's a challenge to grow that amount of money. You don't do it with gifts of $200 or even $500. You do it when you begin to solicit larger gifts. More about that later.

Think about your past work. Did you receive gifts that were much more than the average? Were there donations over a few thousand dollars? What if you siphoned off a portion of those gifts to put into an endowment? Where would its balance be now? And if you haven't gotten gifts of that size, what if you started soliciting for them with the purpose of an endowment in mind? What if you could show a wealthier donor how her gift could last forever with interest funding a scholarship or some other annual cost? Wouldn't that attract more "legacy" gifts?

It takes an evolved fundraiser to see the value in an account that doesn't immediately support their annual operating work. Think of it like an acquisition mailing. This is where you purchase names of people who give to other organizations but not yours. You try to do it intelligently, find those donors who seem to have an affinity towards causes similar to yours. Then you mail information about your organization. Alternatively, you can blanket an entire wealthy zip code, but let's not get bogged down by the details. The results? Usually very poor. You're lucky to get a very small percent of the people to respond. Your return on investment? Suffice it to say it's extremely expensive to buy these lists and do this type of mailing—and normally these projects operate at a loss. It's very hard to sell your board on an acquisition mailing, and I know for a fact it may even be difficult to sell your CEO.

But I have seen the results of acquisition mailings first hand. Somebody who gave $25 years ago – it may have even been a smaller amount – turns around to leave you a five- or six-digit gift in their estate. Still, the big payoff happens generations after you have worked there. So how enthusiastic are you going to be when a board member says, "Why are we doing that acquisition mailing? It's a real loser. Concentrate on approaching our current donors."

The problem: if you're not seeking out new donors, you will have a serious problem in that your current donors don't always stick around. New donors help to protect against current donors lapsing. This has been proven out in the marketplace. An endowment is very similar. It protects against the ebbs and flows of your everyday fundraising. Are you up for the challenge of taking on this type of long-term work even if you're not around after two years? That depends: is this your job or your profession?

Imagine a donor just gave you a seven-digit gift. The only catch: you couldn't use it to meet your obligations for this year. How would that make you feel? How would that make your CEO or Board of Directors feel? With any luck, they're all in agreement and celebrate.

You don't want to leave those circumstances up to chance, there needs to be a plan. There should be a design or rubric for dealing with such an impressive gift. The plan should include a formula for calculating what gets used for today and what gets put aside for tomorrow. Now everyone's happy, most importantly the donor.

There are many fundraisers who say, "Leave the endowments to Harvard. We are not Harvard." I know at least one fundraiser who has said this; that would be me. Over and over again I'd say this. To some extent it was legitimate for me to say. Endowments are best when they're built big. You want the small percent interest you are restricted to using to be on a bigger balance.

But what is a significant payout? If every year you have $5,000 in interest from a smaller endowment, how could you use that? For a small college, that could be five helpful scholarships. For a food cupboard, that may be helpful in paying truck expenses.

And once you begin using a more modest payout from a less substantial endowment, it could attract additional gifts. You don't want to spend all your time soliciting mass amounts of people for smaller gifts – you could begin to solicit donors with more means for larger gifts. All of this to say, "It's all what you make it."

When you're starting an endowment, emphasize the payout that happens each year and stress the fact that it happens each and every year. The payout amount may be much less to start, but your donors will be encouraged by what that helps support each year. Make the most of that payout no matter how modest it is. It is the key to ensuring that you can build that fund for major gifts down the road.

We've talked about the funds and a little about the role of the fundraiser. Now we focus on what the funds are there to help, namely the charity. Does the nonprofit stand on a solid foundation for growth and long-term viability? All three of the funds depend on your nonprofit standing on three unshakable pillars.

# PART III

## *Four Pillars*

*"My work is the only ground I've ever had to stand on. I seem to have a whole superstructure with no foundation, but I'm working on the foundation."*

Marilyn Monroe

No matter who your nonprofit serves, there are four pillars that support the work you do. Like the legs of a table, compromise one and stability is at risk. The four pillars are: structure, community, leadership, and the most important pillar of them all, hope. Structural integrity answers the question: how do we get things done? Community gives your mission a sense of village and your donors, leaders, and beneficiaries a feeling of kinship. Leadership focuses on who helps you get things done and how you lead in the field. And for the fourth pillar, you answer the most important questions: how do we make our world a better place and why do we do what we do?

These four are not interchangeable but they are interrelated for certain. They reinforce one another because, well... they are supposed to be pillars. Neglect one, and the nonprofit may still function but in an unstable way. How the work gets done is as important as the community that benefits. How you lead is tied to why you're in business.

The idea of the four pillars came to me while I was reading about the early Christian Church in the Book of Acts (yes, the one in the Bible). These elements were in the early Church, which has withstood centuries of scandals and schisms and revolutions from within. There is something to be said for the longevity of Mother Church. Is it perfect? Do you really have to ask? It's made out of people – and no matter how guided it is by something greater than itself, it's still led by people, who are imperfect. Is it even "nonprofit" when you see the wealth it has accumulated? This book doesn't tackle that debate. All I'm saying is that I based these four pillars from those that held up the early Church. So as imperfect as it is, complete with disgraces and splinters over the ages, the Church endures.

Could these four pillars be used with for-profit institutions? Any company can benefit from spending some time understanding whether it makes the grade on any of these. And it's not as simple as knowing your product and knowing your customer. I'm assuming you've spent some time understanding these. This dives in a little deeper to uncover the motivators of your business. You're the salesperson, and it's the business, might as well get to know its motivation better.

# CHAPTER 7

## *Structure, the First Pillar*

Structure is the way work gets done at your organization. And here I'm not talking about the fundraising area. You learn that on the job quickly and spend the next few years refining and revising that system. No, I'm talking about the entire organization's operations, facilities, programs, and budget. The most common mistake many new fundraisers make is not studying the way things other than fundraising work at their nonprofits. Until you understand how boxes move, beneficiaries are served, and budgets are balanced, you're at a disadvantage when speaking to donors. That's true no matter if you're reaching out through direct mail, on social media, or one-on-one.

How do you do what you do? Not how do you raise money. How does your organization serve? Let's look at a food bank. How does it move food? How does it procure food? How does it build on its essential mission, namely to make sure food gets into the hands of people who need it? How about a nonprofit theater? How many people came to the latest production? More importantly, how was that leveraged for advertising or sponsorships? Or an animal welfare group. Pretty simple work one would think, right? Save dogs and cats by finding them new families. But talk to an animal lover and see right away how complicated it can get. How are populations (mostly cats) controlled? How do you leverage what you do for funding because, hate to break it to you, you're probably never going to make enough on adoption fees?

What is your product? "We're a nonprofit," some would say, "We don't have products." That's like saying you're a nonprofit so you don't have to make a profit. Every nonprofit should budget for a surplus every year. Try doing it the other way and let me know how long you stayed in business. Likewise, you have a product. Food banks give away meals, theaters produce shows, and animal shelters give pets a new home. But in actuality, food banks show compassion, theaters inspire expression, and shelters help us all be more humane. You're selling something all right.

In short, you should be well-versed in the way your organization budgets and spends its money and not only how you raise it. If you don't concentrate on this, you run the risk of not being in control of the one thing you're supporting – namely, the daily work of your organization.

If you're not in command of what's going on operationally, sit down with your COO or director of facilities or some other such person who manages logistics. Sit with the team that dishes out the meals or teaches the financial literacy workshop or helps with homework after school. Spend some time on the front lines. Not too much time, after all you do have to raise money, but enough time to really get a flavor for the delivery of your mission and an appreciation of the details. The devil is in the details? No, the spirit for what you do is in the details. The devil only wants you to miss the details.

It's in these discussions with your operations staff that you may find where structural unsettledness may be. No, you can't fix everything, but it's good to be in the know. Your logistics team will tell you where the system may be failing. You may hear, "Well, this should be happening but it's not." Or maybe, "This team should be doing this or that, I don't know why they don't do it." Again, you can't fix it all, but tuck it away. You may want to bring up those insights later.

You never know when a complaint from an operations or programs person may turn into the basis for a grant application. Or you may speak with a donor who has experience in a particular program, and your question from the facilities team may be a great question to ask in getting to know them.

Employee handbooks, policies and protocols, even safety guides may not be the most exciting things to speak about, but when neglected, the very foundation of the nonprofit can erode. How long can a food pantry last if safe handling rules are ignored? Can a theater thrive if its season doesn't adhere to a schedule? Does an animal rescue have a chance if the pets are unkempt when possible families come to visit?

For fundraisers, the most frustrating operational shortcoming is if there is little or sloppy data kept by the program people regarding people served or whatever indicators show how well services are being provided. Invariably, there will be a grant provider who wants to see the number of people served and a breakdown of their ethnicity, gender, age, etc. The first time you ask for this data from the program staff, you'll learn right away where the pitfalls in data collection exist. You could wash your hands of it and tell your supervisor that the staff needs to improve in this area. Or you can be the person to call that meeting and get everyone on the same page to preserve the funding. You lose that grant, and it's that much more work on your end to make up for it next year.

If you think structural integrity is the responsibility of others in your organization, you're right. If you think you don't need to do something about any flaws in that structure, you're wrong. A house built on shifting sand cannot stand. A nonprofit without sound operational practices may survive, but it will struggle to thrive. You can find ways to bring up suggestions to the leadership team. With the right leadership in place, you can fix what is not working. If you're unsure about leadership, well that's a whole other problem.

Structure, logistics, the inner workings—call it what you want. If you don't have a strong grip on this, how can you possibly build a community, cultivate leadership, or offer a vision for the future?

# CHAPTER 8

## *Community, the Second Pillar*

Remember the saying, "It takes a village to raise a child?" It was made popular by a book from Hillary Rodham Clinton in 1995, when she was First Lady. Her assertion (in summary): there are a number of influences in a child's life in addition to immediate family. At the time, some argued against her (usually along party lines) that the immediate family was of utmost importance. Whatever your take, I can say "it takes a village to make a nonprofit operate." Can anyone argue with that?

Your community is the village that helps get your work done, the donors who help pay for it, the team that leads efforts, the elected officials who can offer support, and beneficiaries who benefit from your services. Everyone works together as your nonprofit's community. As a group, they become the "soul" of what you do, the migration of effort, the embodiment of encouragement. They are the sweet older couple who faithfully attend your special events. They are also the beneficiaries who receive your services, get back on their feet, then return to volunteer. These are the good will stories that excite people about your cause.

Here are the essential groups within your community:

-Staff: this is the team that gets it all done on the front lines. There may be a few, there may be many.

-Board: here are the volunteers who plan and strategize and keep an eye on the books.

-Donors: those who give to the cause, attend events, or volunteers who give of their time.

-Civic groups and leaders: local charity groups, maybe local churches, schools, and elected officials.

-Community-at-large: those people who may not give or volunteer, but they see what you're doing all the same.

I worked a soup kitchen. It was an amazing place. What started out as a meal for people in need became a society unto itself. It had a medical clinic, legal office, art class, social service office, as well as a place for people to wash their clothes and get a shower. If you were living alone on the street, it was like having family to visit. It was a magnificent village.

What was really amazing was the sense of community that built up around this soup kitchen. It started with caring people who made casseroles and froze them to be served at any time from the kitchen. Then there were people who helped serve the meals. Or how about attorneys who freely gave of their time to help people recover birth certificates or other essential documents. The social worker helped with utilities, housing, daycare, and other issues. The nurses took blood pressure and other screenings to help identify health risks. It was an astounding work done by what seem to be an army of helpers.

And the beneficiaries helped too. Once people came for a meal, they would maybe help in the garden to grow vegetables or in the art class to be a teaching assistant. Have you ever asked, "How can my beneficiaries become volunteers? How can they help?" Maybe you think about that, and the first thing that comes to your mind is that you aren't sure how that would work. I'm not saying every beneficiary needs to become a volunteer. All I'm saying is that when you have a standout volunteer who was at first a beneficiary – well that is a fantastic story to tell any donor and more importantly one who can give substantially.

It all comes back to community. This is absolutely in your hands as a fundraiser. You are the one who builds through donations, events, and a volunteer base. Volunteerism is one of those lead-off conversations you could have with a potential donor. From the frontlines to sitting on the Board of Directors, there are ample opportunities for volunteers to get involved. This engages the community.

Think about the community you serve. This goes beyond the beneficiaries who come to your door or your neighborhood. Imagine the story you can tell to the entire region where you perform your services. You help the region become more humane in whatever service you're providing. How do you communicate that to the community at large? How do you message the value you bring?

As you build your community, your donors and the community-at-large are watching. The ones who can help a little are watching, reading the newsletter, hopefully reading the news because of all the good that you're doing. When you send them that direct mail piece, they should be writing a check. For your donors of more significant means, you call on them to meet up and discuss the work being done. Hopefully, they will engage.

Everybody in your community is important. No, you may not shake each and everyone's hand as a fundraiser. But you can commit to doing your best with the hands you do shake. In the end, you're in the business of building relationships.

Oh, no he didn't do it! He didn't bring up the essential element of fundraising that is used by some as a catchphrase. Building relationships. Well, I did. That is at the center of all we do. But "building relationships" are not just nice words to say. You have to practice the discipline to make the building of relationships a reality

How do you build a village at your nonprofit? Events play a big role certainly. Newsletters and emails do as well. But that's not all of it. Here's where the structure comes into play. What do you do to ensure your staff is completely satisfied and that you earn the reputation of being a world-class place to work? How do you foster an urgency for innovation among your staff, board, beneficiaries, and volunteers as well as donors and civic groups/leaders? You want everyone in on the action to break through to next generation advancements in your service delivery model.

Engage your staff, all of your staff not just the fundraising team. Learn what makes volunteers come back to serve. Tap into the minds of your Board leaders. Seek to understand your beneficiaries. Schedule time to meet with civic groups and leaders. This is how the fundraising department sends out good community vibes.

As your villages engages so your network evolves. There is a gravitational pull to organizations that are busy and innovative. People want to be associated with a nonprofit that commands the issues within the space it operates. Be a thought leader to win their support. Your leadership plays an important part here, and so does your vision. This is the next pillar.

# CHAPTER 9

## *Leadership, the Third Pillar*

There are three core measurements for effective leadership at any nonprofit: how does the board and staff at your nonprofit lead, what is the organization's standing as an authority in its field and within the community at large, and how you (yes, you) lead.

*Staff and Board Leadership.* What motivates executives, managers, and the boards who lead nonprofits? They all may have a vision, they may have passion, but if they don't have an eye on the other pillars, they are failing to see the entire picture. What are some of the characteristics of a good leader? Strategic thinking, mapping goals, and being able to motivate others. Yes, all of these. But what about attention to detail, sensible budgeting, being able to work well with others. Look at today's headlines. Misappropriation of funds, improprieties, sometimes scandalous behavior. These headlines tell of a severe lack of true leadership.

What is a servant leader? It's somebody who knows that their only job shouldn't be walking around telling other people what to do. Instead, they work with others to get things done. Ever know a servant leader? There are plenty of books on the subject. Don't settle for bumper sticker sentiments about servant leadership. There are enough posters with pithy sayings about leadership to fill an entire wall. It means nothing if you don't adopt the philosophy in your heart. Pick up a good book on the subject and have at it.

You have heard leaders say, "I'm here because I believe in the mission." How many times do we believe it? Certainly, they're not in it for the money, right? When you see what some of the leaders at a nonprofit make in salary and sometimes bonuses, you can't always say they're in it for the good but rather the good money.

Sure, every good leader deserves to make a living while they help the cause. There's a popular presentation about how nonprofit leaders don't make the kind of money their counterparts in for-profit companies do. The speaker says it's awful how nonprofit executives are valued so below market. But isn't there a reason for that? Aren't these managers driven by something more than just compensation?

You would think so, but sometimes I'm not so sure. I've seen some leaders in nonprofit organizations with one hand holding the mission statement and another hand holding the latest salary compensation survey. So which do they serve?

Maybe money isn't the motivator; maybe it's prestige or power. Either of those can get you equally as drunk as money. To be the big boss, or to be invited to all the right parties… When these become the end game, maybe those leaders have lost their way.

Politicians will sometimes say it, "I made a sacrifice to serve the people – I could've done much better in private industry." After seeing some of the compensation packages for those in political office, and I mean the complete packages not just salary, I'm not sure I can believe the "sacrifice" argument. And I don't believe it when a nonprofit leader makes similar statements. For a wonderful analysis of this, check out the spring 2019 edition of the Stanford Social Innovation Review for the article entitled, "End Bloated Salaries in the Nonprofit Sector," by Dean Baker.

And what of the Board of Directors? Surely, their commitment is a sacrifice. They give of their time, their talent, and many times their treasure to be on the leadership team. Certainly, they're doing it for altruistic reasons, right? I'm happy to say most times I find this to be the case. They are there because they want to help.

But even with volunteer leaders, their ego can get in the way. For sure, the money doesn't attract them to the job because there is no money. At least there shouldn't be. There is a movement afoot that would convince us board members should be monetarily compensated. Let's ignore these proponents and hope they go away. But what of the prestige? What looks good on their resume? The trip of being the "true boss" of the executive team? These can also be very attractive reasons to want that power position. When you know why a person wants to lead, you'll get a good idea of how they're going to lead. And it's the motivation that makes the biggest difference!

*Challenges of a Long-Term Leader.* Who are the challenging leaders among us? If you're thinking about the ones who go to jail or get fired – well, you're on the right track but not quite. Before these scoundrels make that kind of news, who are they? How can you identify them? You may be surprised to hear that they can sometimes be very effective. In fact, for many years they may carry the weight of the work. They are that motivated. They are possibly even that passionate or compassionate.

This leader will call the shots. They will lead by staying one step ahead of everyone else. They have wonderful ideas, and many times they know how to start them. That's how they got in the spot in the first place. That's how they convinced everyone to more than just listen but also subscribe to their way of thinking. They keep others in check by saying, "That's a great idea, but we tried that a few years ago and it didn't work."

Before you call the person I'm describing a tyrant, think again. This person is almost always beloved. They get things done, they don't wait for others to tell them what to do. And their Board of Directors feel a sense of accomplishment. Look what "we" accomplished. That's what they'll say to you, and you will buy it. Because you're part of a winning team.

Consider it. These people have been at this job a long time. Nobody comes in like this after three months. Normally, they take years to understand the business inside and out. They take years to come up with new ideas and try them out. You forget the ones that didn't work, but you remember the ones that did. They spend years at this. Look at the leader that is pulling everyone else by the nose. How long have they been there? Yes, usually a very long time.

They probably even grew up with the nonprofit, they may have even started it. Now you're dealing with a "founding leader." The organization and its leadership cannot think of life without this person. Or at least they shudder to think of it. Don't think for a second that this leader doesn't realize this.

This works… until they're challenged. It won't come easy. For many years, some may consider an uprising but don't follow through. They won't get the support from the rest of the board. But something happens. Maybe there's a noticeable misstep from the leader. Maybe it's an unbalanced budget. Maybe it's years of deficit spending. Maybe the mortgage goes into distress. Maybe they can't make payroll for one too many periods.

Something happens and somebody says to this leader, "Are you certain the way you're running things is correct?" And the challenger may not be another dynamo, not some other larger than life titan who wants that leader's job or role. In fact, the opposite may be true. They may just be someone with an eye for detail who's peeking behind the proverbial curtain, looking at each line of the budget. They may seem picayune but possibly they're the most important leadership asset you've got.

This challenger may discover faults covered up by the "beloved" leader. Transparency is not one of the glowing traits of these beloved leaders. In fact, they purposefully present the facts as they want them to appear. It is one of the few Achilles' heels that ultimately causes the end of their reign.

What can be other weaknesses of these leaders? We already mentioned lack of transparency. How about an inability to balance the budget. Or here's one for you, may have never guessed this one. How about they get older and want to retire? No matter what, that one is inevitable. Sure, they may have a succession plan. But that next leader they have lined up maybe doesn't have the same charisma. Maybe they don't have a compelling vision (or, worse, none at all).

We have already discussed the detriment of short turnaround time for development professionals. But the opposite is also worthy of warning (although I'm probably only going to say this once here): a leadership position held by one person for decades is not the best approach either. Sure, there's a sense of stability. But also on the leader's part there's a sense of ownership that can become warped. "I've been doing this for more than 20 years, and I'm not going let some newcomer tell me what to do!" I've heard that too many times.

If you see yourself as one of these leaders I'm describing—and I'm not too worried about that self-revelation because most times people don't see it in themselves—you would do well to understand your role in creating something that will last beyond your years. The word organization has as its route the Latin "*organum*." The meaning: instrument, organ. Like an organism. An organization is supposed to be a growing thing, one that takes on new leadership, new expectations, and a new meaning for how it is supposed to serve.

You may have heard it said the best manager works herself out of a job. This simply means they know how to develop the people around them to take on leadership roles (including their own). Begin lining up your succession plan on the first day of your job. And understand the plan includes everybody on your team. It's a collaborative effort. And it comes back to the first pillar. Structure. Make sure you have the best team, the right committees in place, and make sure you're cultivating the kind of volunteer leadership talent that it's going to take to keep things going, even when it's time for you to leave.

And if you're a fellow leader at this organization, the one where the powerful force of one person is guiding everything else, start to speak up. Not in dissension and certainly not in hostility. It's time to speak up about how the nonprofit is going to continue it's good work after that person is gone. You owe it to your organization, the people it serves, and yourself.

*Organization as Community Leader.* What is the organization's leadership role? How much influence does a charity have in general? That depends a lot on how much of a thought leader that nonprofit is in the field it serves and their community at large. And ultimately that determines support and success. It's about attending town hall meetings as well as chamber meetings. It's about finding ways to make a presence in the marketplace of ideas. Do reporters know to call your leadership as a subject matter expert?

"We are a small shop," you tell me, adding, "We do a mighty work, but there's not enough of us to take a leadership role out in the community. That takes time and expertise." Sure, it takes all those things, maybe even some money too. But trying to get more gifts by looking at the sky and holding your hands up as if to say, "Please help," is not effective. You have got to demonstrate your capacity to be exceptional stewards when that money comes in. The organization needs to become a leader.

Truly, one of the best ways to move toward organizational leadership excellence is to be present. Show up. Small shop? Train your volunteer leaders to be present. Be there, but be present. Say something. Express yourselves and how your charity helps. Nobody is looking for an inspirational speech. Most times, what the group wants is someone who can simply carry the conversation. More on "being present" later.

You have undoubtedly heard the word "innovation" thrown around, as in experts saying, "Today's nonprofits need to be innovative." You have to not only believe that, you have to embrace it. Donors give to service providers who are innovative much in the same way a customer will buy products from a company that leads the market. It doesn't mean that you need to come up with new services, but you should be able to deliver on promises in ways that are fresh and exciting.

This is not to say you need to redesign your conference room with beanbag chairs and inspiring wall art, or higher the latest creative thinking guru to talk to staff. Most times, all it takes to be innovative is two simple things: listening and following through. Remember our suggestion to talk with the operations staff about how things get done? Remember when you were going to listen to them complain about how some processes may be archaic? Listening, and trying to figure out how to implement a new way of doing things, might be all you need.

*Your Leadership.* Lastly, let's discuss your leadership role? Have you thrown your hands up in the air saying, "What's the use? A leader is born that way. Either you got it or you don't." Rubbish! In your particular area of work, you have the opportunity to lead. I'm not saying that tomorrow you can turn around and become the president of the country or the CEO of a major corporation. Who wants to do that anyway? And for all I know, you're not even being called to do that. But where you're sitting right now, reading this book, is where you can start to lead. In fact, that might be exactly what your nonprofit needs.

You have a job to do, and at the end of the day you can make that job better. The specific task only you do, remember that one? The one that took three steps to do it and now it only takes two steps because you were bright enough to suggest a seemingly tiny change. That is leadership! That is what's needed in every facet of nonprofit life. If you didn't take a task from three steps to two steps, think about which one you could study now.

Your organization needs to take a leadership role in the field that you're in as well as the community at large. Your leaders need to take more of a command not based on ego but based on serving the common good.

While you're at it, believe that you need to take a leadership role with whatever job you've found yourself.

And now we come to the final pillar, the one that should live on beyond any one leader or staff team or volunteer base.

# CHAPTER 10

## *Hope, the Fourth Pillar*

I love thrift stores. They make the world a better place by recycling all sorts of things to reduce waste. And yes I've picked up a good deal or two in my shopping expeditions. When I asked one store who benefitted from sales, the manager said, "We sell donated goods to send inner-city kids to summer camp." When you're communicating for monetary donations, the camp program means more. The person responsible for the store's fundraising gets this, I'll bet, and maybe she'll write taglines, "We sell goods second hand for kids who need a second chance," or, "We give a change of scene so at-risk kids can have a change of heart." It's more about those kids they serve than it is about keeping the store shelves stocked or even that they help the planet by recycling.

When you're soliciting for really big gifts, it becomes even more about the donor. So our fundraiser may take her copy a step further. Those same taglines have more meaning when the action is placed on the donor. "You buy stuff second hand for kids who need a second chance," it might read. This subtle change places the action on the donors, not the store. Or new copy might go like this, "Your purchases here give a change of scene so at-risk kids can have a change of heart."

The fourth pillar can go by many names. I choose to call it: hope. You can call it "vision" or "promise." These words could be interchangeable. If you're thinking "goals," that may be off the mark. Those are different because they may be more like a task list.

How can something abstract like the concept of "hope" be a pillar for any organization? What is hope, and what does it mean for your charity? Hope is something that most everybody can understand in the nonprofit world. We hope that one day we will find a cure for cancer. We hope that one day we can end homelessness. We hope that one day everybody will have enough to eat.

Don't think for a second that our counterparts in the for-profit world don't know what hope is. They call it the promise. "If you buy our product, your life will be improved," they tell us. In the charitable organization realm, we hold the same promises. We will cure this disease. We will end poverty. It may be foolish to think we can. But we can diminish that disease, reduce that social ill, and lessen they're negative impact in our corner of the world.

If your organization is running without considering what your hope is, take a pause and think about it. Yes, it may be in your mission statement, but it's probably more accurately represented in your vision statement. It's surprising how many charities don't have a vision statement.

The mission statement describes your business and the means by which you'll accomplish your goals. Let's look at a fictional example. "Family First Charity exists to support working families who are at or below the poverty line with services to help them succeed. We do this by providing education, essential needs (like food) and workforce solutions."

A vision statement seeks to define what you hope to accomplish within broader context. Not in terms of eradication, but rather in terms of lessening the burden. "Family First Charity envisions a community where families find support for the struggles they face every day to successfully raise their children to be a positive force in society." That captures the hope of this same charity.

Hope ties in beautifully not only as a fourth pillar but also in the three funds. The annual fund, or operating fund, speaks to your daily, monthly, quarterly, and yearly goals. Certainly, this is why you raise money. To reach so many dozens or hundreds or thousands of people with the services you provide. People's lives will be improved. That's the hope.

Your reserve fund will help to address the shortfalls that occur periodically that hinder or maybe even threaten your organization. You raise that funding to resolve issues and stay on track. With that extra payout from a reserve fund, you have the hope of keeping your organization serving through any temporary crisis.

Your forever fund, your endowment is probably the most elusive of them all. It is the one that will help to keep you meeting the demands of your mission. Create goals for that fund. Maybe it's to start new programs until they can gain their own financial support annually. Maybe it's to offer scholarships. Maybe it's to encourage the younger people in your field with free trips to your annual meeting. No matter how small it is, you can do great things with even a modest payout annually. Which hope does that find speak to? The hope in the future, and the hope of maintaining your charity for years to come.

You are a salesperson, or at least now you understand that you are. So what are you selling out there? Are you selling just the good works that your organization does? Or are you selling the hope of what you can address in the community overall. Are you joining the hope of your charity to the larger promise of what society wants?

Many of us go into work every day and look at our desk or calendar and say, "I hope I can get all this done." And that is the extent of hope that we have for work and organizations. How satisfying is that? Do you leave the end of the day looking at your desk and calendar and wondering, "I hope I can get all that done tomorrow."

Day by day, you advance your work. Do you inspire yourself to advance the promise? Every charity has a promise, but sometimes it can get lost in the daily grind of getting stuff done. You can get comfort in achieving small milestones yet miss the big picture. Baby steps lead to bigger steps for certain. But if you're not thinking about the bigger steps, baby steps is sometimes all you take.

Use your hope statements with a donor. Imagine you're having a conversation with a supporter and you want to talk more strategically. You want them to know that you're a thought leader and that investing a donation with you is as sound as it is progressive. You're talking about the bigger steps, those more monumental dreams you have. And in your heart, you hear a small voice saying, "When was the last time you thought about those bigger steps?"

We're supposed to be thinking and acting strategically, but we get wrapped up in the easier things to do, monitoring other people's work or making sure the department reaches its monthly goal. We forget that we have been put in charge to take a leadership role, and advancing the hope or promise of the organization is part of that charter.

Maybe take a few minutes every day or every other day or a couple days a week. Close your office door. If you don't have one, find a conference room that has one and schedule it out, and close that door. And think. Or watch a video. Stand on that balcony, as my favorite boss would say. Look at all the moving parts, and ask yourself how you can invigorate the hope your organization has for its own advancement and society at large. And get to work on plotting or planning or designing.

Write a reminder in your calendar today to do this, and don't mark it as complete until you've taken one step in that direction. Then place another reminder on your calendar in a week or two to look at this again. If an audacious goal is not on my calendar, it will not get done.

## PART IV

## *Demystifying Major Gifts*

*"Just remember this, Mr. Potter. That this rabble you're talking about...they do most of the working and paying and living and dying in this community."*

George Bailey *from the film*
It's a Wonderful Life

If you're going to grow revenue beyond your annual fund, you must start thinking of how to grow major gifts. You have other revenue streams: special events (like galas or Coach Bingo), direct mail campaigns, direct mail, and grants. All of these are important, but for the most part they are best suited to grow your annual fund, not transform your budget. Major gifts can transform your budget. Why do we ask certain donors to make substantial gifts? We do it because it's the best way for them to give back. It's an investment in your good works, and more than ever they can receive the tax benefits for a much larger gift. Also important is that these gifts give the donor a chance to give back to the masses who helped built their business (one way or another) in the first place. How do we cultivate these donors? It can be as simple as it is complicated...but it starts simple. The work with these donors is just that... work, and it has to get done, but it is possible. It's not a mystery and it's not rocket science, but it is science more than art. There are five areas to cover in driving any major gift programs: strategy, the working pants principle, calendar of touchpoints, *Shark Tank* lessons, the small but mighty, and the greatest pitfall of all. First things first: what is your strategy?

# CHAPTER 11
## *Strategy for Major Gifts*

It always surprises me how many nonprofits do not think about what they would do with a major gift if they received one. They all fantasize about it, don't get me wrong, but when it comes to actually receiving one, many times there is no real plan. When this happens, a large gift that could transform the organization is often put into the operating account and used up that year (or in a year or two).

There is something inherently wrong in this approach. If a gift of five or six figures comes in, how wrong is it to use that up within a few years? It should have more longevity. Think of the impression staying power of their gift will make on a donor.

If somebody gives that large a gift, and you can demonstrate to them how you plan to use that gift over many years to do amazing work, how more inclined will they be to make another gift of that size and magnitude? And let's say the gift was part of an estate for somebody who had no children nor next of kin. Imagine demonstrating to the community that you plan to use that gift in perpetuity as a legacy in that person's name. What impression does that make on the decedent's friends or neighbors?

The fact is your major gifts program begins with the annual or operating account. That account must be budgeted for and successfully create a surplus every year. The surplus feeds into the reserve account. Surplus is from the reserve account is used as seed money for an endowment. It's a simple design. Then, a major gift comes in and perhaps a small amount is allocated to operating, a little more for reserves, and maybe the bulk is used for the endowment. Imagine reporting back to a donor just how you used her gift—and that some of it will leave a legacy for the nonprofit.

If you don't have a plan for how you're going to use major gifts, then best to not start soliciting until you've talked about it. Draw up a policy, be the mastermind behind a protocol, get your board and executive team excited and involved. The bottom line is that you need to establish a strong operating fund that does not rely on major gifts, and that will feed into a reserve fund, and surplus from the reserve will be seed money for the endowment. It can be determined that major gifts will be allocated to each three of the funds in whatever way you organization feels is necessary. Ideally, that should lean away from the operating fund and more toward the endowment.

The real work in the success of all three funds is in making sure the operating fund remains at a surplus. This requires a lot of forethought in budgeting, intelligence in the forecast analysis design, and making mindful decisions all along the way, some of which may be very difficult. Do you really need that program that doesn't feed directly into your mission? You have five members on the team where only three may be necessary. You've been doing things this way for a long time, but consider doing it that way and you might save money.

Where can automation help to reduce costs? In warehousing or programming. However, even in fundraising. You've been doing your own mailings in-house, but if you worked with a vendor could you actually save money on postage and other hard costs? You may even spend the same amount of money as you would be doing it in-house, but the results may be dramatically improved.

I am painfully aware that keeping your operating account at a surplus requires you to look at your largest expenditure overall: personnel. Nobody wants to talk about staff turnover or having to layoff anybody. However, this is not something you do within weeks. It's something you do over a longer period of time to see if you can take advantage of naturally-occurring attrition or other changes among staff that create opportunities to save money. Staffing decisions are possibly the hardest discussions you need to have. Nobody wants to look like a cutthroat Fortune 500 company when you're operating a small nonprofit. However, there is no way to avoid discussions about this subject.

Here is where leadership plays an integral role. Some leaders enjoy building staff in an attempt to build their own empire. After a few hires, you're wondering how much work there is to go around. Maybe you see the staff structure as bloated. So it's even before staff is hired that you ask the tough questions about who can do this work without hiring somebody new. All of this to say that if you're operating account fails to be at a surplus, you know the first line item you need to examine.

A word about goals. Take a look at what your major gifts outreach has brought in so far this current year. A plan to grow that to 800 times its current size in one to three years is not only unreasonable, it's foolish. Yet I've seen it happen. You can only grow revenue by the dictates of benchmarks in the marketplace. What is the average size of fund growth in nonprofits in your sector and location? That would be a good benchmark. Anyone who wants you to grow higher than the benchmark is trying to use you to build an empire. If you're applying for the job, don't. If you're already in that job, impress upon leadership the need to work with benchmarks. If that doesn't help, you may want to consider a move.

With any luck, you can convince leadership of the need for a good strategy to receive major gifts. Why go through all this work? Let's explore that, one pant leg at a time!

# CHAPTER 12

## *Working Pants*

"Leave the endowments to Harvard," I used to say. As already discussed, it's easy to be skeptical about how such a restricted fund can help the smaller or grassroots charity. Universities, hospitals, and the church – these were the three entities commonly believed to be most capable of cultivating and achieving significant gifts for an endowment. People love giving to their Alma Mater, the hospital that helped save their life or the life of a loved one, or of course in their faith.

"Our small charity is not like a university," many have told me, "where alumni look back after a successful career and want to give to the school that taught them so much." Maybe you help families in a food line. Or you rescue dogs and cats. Or treat addicts. Where is our alumni? Who are the people looking back with such strong affinity with an ability to give a five- or six-digit gift? So do we throw up our hands in defeat?

Not so fast. Eventually in every nonprofit, a leader wants to start a major gifts program. It could be a board member or executive manager who hears about the larger gifts other charities in the field are getting, and they want a piece of the action. Here is where your troubles can begin, both in starting such a program or not knowing how to receive those more significant gifts should you get one.

What is the most basic rule of major donor solicitation (or really any sales task)? Know your customer. Well...yes and no. Is that the root element of a major gifts program? How about this: Have a plan. That gets closer. Without context for your major gifts program, you've only got a pretext. So put it in context. How do you do that? Of course, the answer is in the why, as in "Why do we want to start a major gifts campaign?"

If you think it's the money, I'm not sure you'll be completely satisfied. This is a difficult program to start let alone keep going. If you think you're just going to bolster this year's giving, what happens when you want to approach the same donor in a couple years and ask for more? "What did you do with the gift I sent last time," they might ask. Sure, it's about money, but it can't all be about that. What is it? Your mission? Your programs? Your beneficiaries?

How about this: why not make it about the donor? This is the chance of a lifetime for your donor to give back in a big way. Give back to whom? To the ones who gave so much to them as they were building their business—like customers or policy holders, or retailers.

Enter the working pants. My maternal grandfather, who I never met, supposedly said as he walked into any beautiful church – especially the one he attended in South Philadelphia, *"Pantaloni."* What he meant, or at least the way my mother interpreted her father's Italian, was this, "The working pants built this church."

He didn't mean the masonry. He wasn't referring to the drywall or the flooring. Although it was in all likelihood the "working pants" did most of that work on all those buildings, but it's not what my grandfather meant.

He meant the donations.

Not the donations from church goers in that particular neighborhood as it was a working class part of town. It was broader than that. In collections throughout the city and throughout the world, the church was able to do its good work. In a very real sense, each donation built the capacity of the institution.

Let's scale my grandpop's idea. When you think about it, every business starts with the working pants paying for goods and services. With every loaf of bread they purchase, with every movie ticket they buy, with every gallon of gas they put in their cars, with every online subscription, they build the revenue base. That, in turn, moves the gears that generate profits and staff work and executives, and ultimately the upper class.

For certain the business person found perhaps a better way to fill the consumer's need, that ability to take advantage of the supply and demand formula. But just as certain, the working pants swipe their cards or lay their money down to buy. You'll hear sometimes, "That was a great idea, but it just never took." But if you have that great idea, and the conditions are right... a company or invention has a hit on its hands.

The big boss can argue that when something larger is at play in the company's good fortune, then stars align and "the universe is favoring you." For me, that's God shining a light on your idea and allowing it to flourish. The working class begins to buy, the money collects, and it swims upstream. If that's been a "blessing," then give because of your faith. If you think the universe is being kind, keep that karma in motion by giving back. Either way, give back.

For some industries, it may be a little difficult to envision the success of their business with average citizens throwing a dollar down to buy (for example) medical malpractice insurance. But if you think long enough about how those industries are built, it doesn't take long to draw the line between that business and the working pants who all make it possible. Patients get sick, now you need to buy malpractice insurance.

Take the time to trace it back. The wealthy donors who have made it a point to increase their philanthropy know what I'm talking about. They know that the meals they eat (out or in, doesn't matter), beds they sleep in (at home or away), or miles they travel are all made possible by the working pants. And those families, their children, their aging parents—they struggle. There are charities that care, so those wealthy donors give.

Because they know it's only right.

As fundraisers, as the salesforce for just causes, we are the ones to remind those who can help about the need to give back to those who got them there. Barbara Ehrenreich wrote a book entitled *Nickel and Dimed: On (Not) Getting by in America*. Barber is a journalist who spent many years undercover, working low-paying jobs and living on those wages. She found it dramatically challenging. Here are some final observations in her book:

It may be easy to forget the working class, as Ehrenreich points out. They sometimes can fade into obscurity. They become the people emptying the trash that we do not see. They become the housekeepers we do not hear. She says in her book, "The 'working poor' ...are the major philanthropists of our society" because they do most of the work to make our lives more convenient. In fact, she adds, they may feel themselves marginalized because they do not see themselves mirrored in TV where it would seem most characters on sitcoms make $15 or more. Her book is a fascinating read, and I highly recommend it.

Fundraisers are really the advocates for the working class, sometimes we pose as beggars. We work to remind those who have done well in their careers and finances that there must be a place in their budget for the causes that help people who are less fortunate. Not only for the colleges that taught them or the hospital that healed them, but for everyone.

It's what separates us from the animal kingdom. The ability to reason. When you have reason, you can't help but evolve in your thinking to reject "survival of the fittest." At times, you've got to compete and exert your championship attitude. At other times, you must give back to help those in need. We don't simply approach the weak in society and tell them to "get a job." You've got to feel their pain and open you heart and hands to help.

Imagine if every multi-millionaire considered that every event ticket, every pair of socks, every cell phone subscription added up to their seven- or eight-digit salary. And instead of hearing of these celebrities or celebrity business people buying another luxury home or adding a race car to their collection, they gave an additional 10% of their fortune to charity. Imagine how much good could be done in the world. "Why should I give more away?" they may ask. "It's live or let die out here. We're all just in a pecking order, and I just happen to be on top. I give my due to charity."

Thankfully for so many wonderful causes, there are other donors who acknowledge their own good fortune, they do remember, and they do give back bigger than the average gift. For these donors, there are opportunities to make transformative gifts. It's our job as fundraisers to encourage that and to build the system to receive those gifts and steward them properly. We're here to remind people why they should be philanthropic what blessings that will give for them and their entire family and community.

Now that we know why we are asking donors to give more substantially and what we're going to do when we when we receive those gifts, let's meet one of my favorite benefactors.

# CHAPTER 13

## *Meet Jane Doe*

Now that you know why you're reaching out, and how to best receive that funding, do you know the donors who can make a significant gift? Have you got a plan for how you will reach out? As mentioned, you can get wealth overlay data. Before you spend a lot of money, see if your central library or a regional nonprofit support center has access to a resource to help. Some have that database for use gratis. And if you get that data, you may want to spot check it. Sometimes data like that is comprised of very wild estimates. Let's say you've gone through, and you're staring at 50-100 names on a spreadsheet. Everything may or may not be there. Names, addresses, phone numbers, emails. What now? First, let's get to know each and every name on that list. That process starts with just one.

Meet Jane Doe. I always talk about Jane. She's the kindest person. Very philanthropic and has her heart in the right place. Of course, she's completely imaginary, my way of speaking about donors in general. Hopefully, you've split the list so that you know Jane, she is a current supporter or may not but separately is a prospect. You know the number of times she's given to your cause, when the last time was, and how much she's given overall. If that amount is already high, you know she is a friendly donor. You should also know if Jane has volunteered with you or not. Has she ever visited for a tour before?

Now you have Jane Doe's information on how much she is able to give. The first thing to remember is: Jane may not at all like the fact that you were able to retrieve her personal data so quickly. Don't ever mention your report to Jane. And if you know Jane made a gift to another organization like yours, of course you don't ever bring that up. That's not important, and she may be offended about how much you know. "What are we supposed to do now that we know about Jane?" you ask. Simple. For now, simply know the information. Where we go from here may surprise you.

Let's find out who knows Jane. You ask your board or other leaders. It is invariably preferred to get a warm introduction through someone who knows her. You may have to dig a little, don't stop at the board. Maybe after a little research, you find Jane is a member of a certain club (like a tennis club). One of your committee chairs is also a member of that club. There may be any connection worth exploring. No matter if you get a connection or not, you need to begin reaching out.

Do you call or mail them? The answer is, "Yes but don't overdo it!" Mail her a personal note. Handwritten is best, or typeset with a handwritten P.S. The more customized the better. And follow up with a phone call a few days later, hopefully they hear your voice after they have received your note.

It can't be emphasized enough that if you do a lot of direct mail, you should consider taking Jane off that list or have her on but for only a once or twice per year. This way, she receives less mail asking for a smaller gift. You're looking for a five- or six-digit gift, but your mailer probably asks for up to $500. That's sending the wrong message.

You're sending a note, what should you ask? Do you ask her, "Can we spend a few minutes talking about how you can support our programs?" No. Bad form. How about, "Jane, we wanted to reach out to simply say thank you for all of your support." That's nice, but maybe a little too soft. The best approach when reaching out to Jane is to ask, "Can I get your advice?" Jane has an interest in you as a leader in the field, and you should have an interest in her as a person whose opinion counts.

Advice about what? How about advice on your new strategic plan? Better still how about asking her input as you build that plan. You can ask, "Are we on the right track?" Or you may ask, "Is there anything we missed? Would you see us doing anything differently?"

There is nothing that gives another human being more ownership in your own welfare than asking them for their advice about something. Strategic plan already built? Ask them their advice about implementation. Not built yet? Ask them to a special session with other prominent leaders to get their opinions.

Of course you can't change the direction your board wants to take with regard to a strategic plan every time you're enjoying coffee with a potential major donor. However you can bet that board will want to hear what their donor said.

You can also ask about that complicated challenge being faced by nonprofits in your field? Hopefully, it isn't a scandal, but if it is use it. You could ask, "How can we keep the good works you're interested in moving forward despite the controversy going on?" It may be government cutbacks or an epidemic that's started.

How frequently should you try to reach out? The answer is "at exactly the right frequency." Reach out too many times and you run the risk of getting a "go away" gift. You know, a gift that is generous but not the transformative gift you were hoping to receive. Calling too frequently is normally a result of not having enough accounts in your portfolio. The fewer people to call the more times you'll call each one. When you have a robust pipeline, you don't get hung up on calling any one person.

He was a predecessor of mine at a job I held recently. He called on one particular donor far too many times. In the end, the donor told my CEO to never have him contact her again. She had given tens of thousands of dollars to the cause with large gifts year after year. Sure, that's why my predecessor called on her. When I came on board, I learned about the overzealous outreach and immediately took action. I placed her on once per year mailing, sent her one final personal note to apologize, and wrote her a personal note only once per year. When last I checked, she had still not written back.

But what about starting a campaign and not contacting frequently enough? With less frequent communication, you could lose traction (or fail to get enough of it) toward that coveted sit down cup of coffee. Calling less frequently is usually a result of not placing future actions on a calendar. The act of relationship building is a journey with milestones, and it must be recorded, tracked and on your calendar.

Touchpoints can include personal notes, phone calls, emails, or texts. It can also be meeting with donors at an event you know they'll attend. Galas, chamber receptions, and special events in a field of interest are all good examples. You can easily start to learn the functions that attract the right mix of donors, the trouble is you can't possibly attend them all. It's good to build a calendar of these events, and ask you Board of Directors if they're attending any of them. This way you have an opportunity to perhaps get a list of attendees from them ahead of time and ask if they can seek out some of the people that are on your list.

Let's look at the different strategies to engage Jane, now that we know who she is.

# CHAPTER 14

## *Calendar of Touchpoints*

When it comes to engaging major donors, it's important to find ways to reach them. A calendar of touchpoints or outreach is helpful. This assists you in marking the times you plan to reach out to the donor. Every week or month, there should be new chances or reasons to reach out.

Certainly, invitations for coffee or asking for their insights on a strategic plan are good starts. But what happens when they don't respond because people are busy, and they can't always respond? In fact, if they respond 5% of the time that's big news. Each campaign should net a new 5%, and we consider that wonderful connection activity.

When you're inviting donors to events, we're not talking big galas. An event may be to visit your place or tour a location where you serve people. Or it could be VIP access to an event already being hosted. Having a volunteer day? A special ceremony? And what of the rest of the calendar? Are there community events that will engage donors? Invite them.

My CEO was at an event hosted on our behalf by a major insurance company. Of course, I invited all the donors in my portfolio. A few actually showed up. One of those sweet people turned to my CEO and said, "We always get a call from your staff to join us, we're so glad we could make this event." The boss was thrilled, we all were. I invited that couple for a tour of the facility the following week and pitched a special gifting opportunity, and they donated.

Tours of your place or service sites are great touchpoints? There are so many others that you may not even think about. Once per month or once every other month, think about a reason to reach out, then make that call. Of course, you should be cautious about overextending your outreach. As mentioned before, a donor can feel a little too bombarded by constant phone calls.

Ultimately, you want the donor to visit or be visited. When that happens, you may think they're ready for "a big ask." It's possible but may not be the case. On the first visit, you may want to simply let them know what the next steps will be in connecting with them further. When you visit the next time, be sure your list of products are at the ready. More on that later.

Your first outreach is not all one-on-one and all your letters aren't handwritten. Eventually, however, it does come down to a phone call and setting up a time to speak. As you're preparing for a mailing to every donor, you should know each piece that's going out to your major prospects, because remember it's going to be in the tens not the hundreds. Does "John" like to be called "Jack?" Are you using the right address or do they have a separate address in the winter or summer. As you begin to understand your portfolio, you'll know these subtle differences. Have your mail house send the letter, but know who you will be calling next week when the piece gets to their mailbox.

Not everybody likes to come to events. Everyone may not be able to make it to a tour. But everyone has a passion for some element of your cause, they wouldn't have given otherwise. Maybe you're starting a qualitative research project, and you hope to interview the donor to find out why they give to your cause specifically. This will give you invaluable insights, and it doesn't immediately involve asking them for a gift.

If the person doesn't want to come to events, or they don't want to visit, or they can't talk via phone, do you give up on them? What do you think I'm going to say? You never give up on a donor. Never, never, never. They may not have been interested in an idea or a meeting or special tour… but that doesn't mean they're not listening. If you have a direct mail campaign to your complete list, you may want to pull back on what you send your own portfolio of donors. Not that you don't send them anything, but you send them targeted information.

Instead of sending donors a mailer every month or other month (as you send to your big list), you may want to send "impact reports." Like a newsletter, these reports have maybe a little more tailored information about how their support had an impact on your beneficiaries. You may want to send "strategic plan updates" about how your strategies are paying off for the community you serve. All the while, you're leading up to asking for a significant gift.

Do you know your donor's birthday? Maybe send a card, Yes, that's a touchpoint. Are they interested in your children's program? Is there a good news story you're sending to the press or posting on social media about this program? Why not send the message to your donors who may care? There needs to be a reason to write them, it needs to be on your calendar to send that message.

Until you get to know the donor well enough where they are completely connected to your cause, you need to be disciplined about outreach. Is it tedious to keep a calendar? As tedious as it is to keep raising money for your operating fund year after year. Find ways to attract the more transformative help your donors are willing to provide.

As you reach out to the donor consistently but not overwhelmingly, you eventually gain a share of mind (as the jargon goes). But to what end? What is your goal? If you're looking to put a new addition on your building, isn't that an apparent objective? You build the argument, provide the details, and make a case for the addition. Then you ask. Be the architect of your own perpetual fund that will help maintain the work you do. You're going to need a product. Time to pitch, which only reminds me of one thing: my time in the *Shark Tank*!

# CHAPTER 15

## *Lessons from* Shark Tank

So many things I've learned in business, I learned on *Shark Tank*. For those who don't know, *Shark Tank* is a show where five rich investors sit panel style facing a set of double doors. From down a hallway, hopeful entrepreneurs open those doors to stand in front of the "sharks" to pitch a product or service.

I watched that show for six seasons straight. Apart from watching a lot of television growing up, this is my longest streak watching a show than any other. It's not like I don't know television shows (especially the ones that rise to the top of pop culture), it's just that I don't watch episode after episode of one particular series—except one. *Shark Tank*.

Some of the biggest lessons in business play out with the sharks. First, know your product inside and out, and know the numbers surrounding your product. If your service numbers dropped, know why. If your budget didn't balance last year, be able to speak eloquently about that too. Have an understanding and reason for every twist and turn your organization and its programming have taken over the past few years. And be able to articulate where you see your business going.

Most importantly, understand why you see a future for your service. What are the market conditions for your cause: increase in joblessness, decrease in stay-at-home parents, economic challenges? Know the market and community in which you operate and how it got to where it is, and then how you plan to help.

Know your field. Know your competition. Don't have competition? Believe me, you have competition. Maybe not in your community for exactly what you do, but your competition is asking the same donors you're approaching, so know who gives to the causes that are like yours.

The biggest criticism for *Shark Tank* from some is that they take your idea and half of your business. The sharks may take your idea (and maybe even half the money), but there's a reason. They're sharks! They've navigated in these waters before, and they know how to make sure your product doesn't get swallowed up. They can get you into the right outlets, retail or wholesale. They can get you to the right suppliers who can get your costs down. In other words, they have the relationships necessary to do more with your product. Can you get your gizmo in that major retail chain? The sharks can get you there faster. You can benefit from what and who the sharks know.

Think of your major donors as the sharks. They're not donating to you, they are investing in your work. Your rank-and-file donor is an investor too but in smaller measure. They can't burst into your board meeting and complain about something you're doing wrong. A major donor may pull you aside a cocktail party and say something about how you're doing business.

The two biggest lessons I learned from *Shark Tank* came not from watching the show but from my actually auditioning! Yes, the show's producers were in Philadelphia, and I was working for a food charity that made its own product. We were rescuing food from farmers and making into a shelf stable condiment. Simple enough. I thought maybe the sharks would be interested in the value of the product based on how we were helping farmers, rescuing food, selling the product to fund our other charitable works. We were being social entrepreneurs.

After spending a few hours in a waiting room, it was my time to talk to a screener. How exciting! There were people all around me with crazy gizmos and business plans. Surely, my product would impress them. There were all types of inventors around me. We all waited in the line patiently. It was like an episode of Antiques Roadshow but for entrepreneurs.

It was my turn at last. I walked up to the screener. She was kind enough as she looked at the product and listened to my pitch. She seemed mildly impressed with a dose of skepticism. As she handled the jar, read the label, she listened about how the manufacturing of the product saves farmers tens of thousands of dollars in disposal fees for the perfectly good product we rescue from them.

She had one question for me. Can you guess what it was? "You're a nonprofit," she said quickly, "how do the sharks make money?" My answer was quick, having seen six straight seasons and dozens of episodes.

"We can make arrangements for this as a separate business and start to scale it," I said.

Her answer was swift. "No, it's not for the sharks." She handed me back the jar. That was it. I was dismissed. But therein lies two largest lessons I've learned from the *Shark Tank*. Be in front of the right investors and know how to value your business.

"We're a cause," you say. "We don't sell a product." Certainly, helping people isn't a product. But if there are enough people who need to be helped—and you've developed a system by which they can be helped— then you have a product. Like an after school program that requires supplies and snacks. Or a facility that needs upkeep. Or needing trucks or warehouses to deliver and distribute groceries.

When considering what your product is, think about why you do what you do. We touched on this before. You serve meals to the homeless, but maybe you also try to get them other kinds of help. Are you trying to break the cycle of homelessness? Are you working to build a support network for the most marginalized?

Take a look at what you do and reflect on how deep it can explain it. It's the basis of you valuation. There was a music festival, one that attracted thousands of kids using hip music with a positive message. They were pitching themselves as an arts festival. But really they were in youth development, a second mission, although some would say primary. In discussions with this nonprofit, we learned they would ask musicians to stay on a day or so after the show to speak with students at schools nearby for more positive reinforcement. The case for this "festival" being a youth development platform was built stronger with this update. We went on to discover this group was planning student retreats in conjunction with the festival and trying to find ways to rent busses to get more kids to the show from underserved parts of the city.

In *Shark Tank*, entrepreneurs put a value on their business. That is translated to how much money sharks need to invest to get a certain share of the business. Sure, donors are making a different kind of investment, but don't think for a second they don't get "shares" of your work. Their dividends rest in the hope they have in the longevity of their gift. Value your work and ask for that investment.

How do owners value their businesses? Usually, they do it with a little math and a lot of emotion, too much of the latter. The result: they evaluate too high. The sharks ask the entrepreneur how much in sales her product made in the previous year. Let's say it was $100,000. More importantly, let's say she thinks it will make that in the next year for reasons she's outlined in great detail. If she wants to offer an investor a 10% share, she should ask for $10,000. With that investment, she could grow the sales and that shark gets a 10% stake of the business as it grows.

But for some people in the tank, they value their business far too high. Sales last year were $100,000, and they are offering a 10% share for $20,000. That means the business owners think the business is worth

$200,000. If there is not a compelling reason why the business will not double in the next year, the sharks need to offer $20,000 for a 20% share. This returns the valuation back to $100,000. Many times, the sharks need to offer either less in money or more market share to make the deal.

With your donors, your biggest investors, you need to know the value of your business. But it all can't be driven by emotion. Sure, you help children, seniors, or families. You may bring the arts to people with disabilities who need to express themselves. Whatever the case, making the emotional valuation of your business is the easier part.

The more difficult part is coming up with the outputs you have: how many people did you serve? These are the quantitative numbers that you likely collect. Now is time to analyze those numbers to make a more impactful statement. Having a handle on the impact of your nonprofit today gives you insights about how much more help you can provide in the future, with your major investor's help.

Your donor is an investor. Your fundraiser is a salesperson. Your nonprofit is a business that can't lose money year after year or it will be out of business.

Starting to get real, right?

# CHAPTER 16

## *Small but Mighty*

One of my favorite Shakespeare plays is *A Midsummer Night's Dream*. That's mainly because of an amazing production in which my daughter appeared, okay so I might be biased. She masterfully played Hermia, who is at the center of confusion among a group of young characters falling in and out of love with one another. One of my favorite lines from the play is when Hermia's lover, Lysander (also amazingly played), says about her, "Though she be but little, she is fierce."

You say you're a small shop, and it's difficult for you to get involved in major gift solicitation. I've worked in big departments and little shops. When your resources are limited, you need to constantly evaluate what you're doing to make sure you don't burn out the few people that you have. You have to assess everyone's skill level and determine exactly what new work you can add.

Building your presence among major donors is clearly not simple work. It takes hours of disciplined outreach with progressive touchpoints like personal notes and more. You can't just start it up without figuring out what needs to be adjusted out of your current workload. What are all the steps you're taking now to get your job done? Can that be made easier and free up some time?

Why not start small? You may roll your eyes at this idea, but bear with me. Are you folding your letters before you send them out? For relatively little cost, you can ask your printer to fold the pieces before sending them to you. And while you're at it, can they stuff the envelopes as well. While you're sending out those letters to hundreds or thousands of people, can the return envelope go to a lock box that is directly handled by the bank, who can process checks and send you reports. An important note: I wouldn't recommend a third party be involved in the gift processing, only an actual bank for what should be obvious reasons.

Once you pick apart your processes and look at the mechanics of how things are getting done, you will invariably find ways to streamline and make what your small office is doing more efficient. The bottom line: there is time that can be freed up. Time saved can be spent cultivating relationships with major donors.

Small shop? That's exactly what you need! The smaller the shop, the closer your team can be to those major donors. I guarantee you if you looked long enough you would find that someone from your team (or past staff member) has had a conversation with a major donor. In one case, there was the story of a woman who befriended a donor who called over the phone for a simple change to an address. She engaged the donor, not because she knew who the donor was but just…because. The two hit it off and the donor called back a few more times after to chat further. The bottom line: that donor gave the organization a six-figure gift from her estate. There was another woman who would send donors in our database a birthday or anniversary card each and every year. She didn't do this because they were major donors but only… because. That kind of personal touch gives your cause a human face, kindness and caring you sometimes can't get from larger organizations. Though you be small you can be fierce.

Do you argue that because your office is so small there isn't an expertise in many critical areas of fundraising and philanthropy? All the more reason to seek help from the donors who have been more consistently giving to your cause. Remember, you're in partnership with this special group of donors.

The whole theory and practice of major gifts is small. Personal notes, not high design direct mail campaigns. One-on-one for coffee, not a gala for hundreds with raffles and silent auctions. You may need the other things (direct mail, a gala) to help you identify that 5% of your donor base that can help you with a transformative gift. But when it comes to that finite, small (but mighty) list of donors, you can start to get to know them by a simple act of getting it touch.

Remember niche marketing? Remember when that was a thing? Like when you see a beer or bank billboard ad and they're calling out the home city in which you live. "Hey, Philly, we love your cheesesteaks, and we want to be your bank." And the billboard has a picture of a cheesesteak. Yes, that's sort of like niche marketing. I've seen this done well, and I've seen it done poorly, like when an ad depicts a soft pretzel obviously pandering to the image of our city.

Niche marketing is what we do with major donors. To get them to know you, there must be even more targeted marketing. Call it "micro" marketing. The only impression you may make on these busy donors is your logo on the envelope your personal note comes in. They may even throw out that note most times, but the logo registers. It's like they saw it on a billboard, right in their mailbox. You have to count that as a win and impression you've made, no matter how small it is.

While we're talking about "impressions," one word of caution about online marketing. Certainly, it's effective in that its cost is relatively low for what it can deliver. But you're in a dangerously vast ocean of digital messaging when you solely rely on online marketing. It can easily be missed. If your email is a donor list of 50 people, why wouldn't you personalized each and every subject line? Aren't we all a little desensitized to email marketing these days? We're so numb to it there's even a special folder exclusively to capture all the emails that even appear like a solicitation. They even took away a name from a perfectly good meat substitute for it. You don't want to be labeled a "spammer" so easy because of your digital marketing.

Still thinking the gala is a way to meet people, try a Jeffersonian Meal instead. What is that? President Jefferson, yes that Jefferson, had these meals at his home. He'd invite up to maybe 10-12 people and kept the party size that small on purpose. They'd share a meal, and he'd get them to talk about one topic in particular. It could have been the arts, literature, world affairs, science, or whatever. He made sure the invitees had an expertise in the subject, or at least a strong interest in it. And they would talk. In the process, they got to see insights and views that were much deeper than if they'd had a symposium.

Which setting do you think you'd get to know a major donor more personally, one where there was 100 people attending or one where there were 10 around one table? And if you've got a small office, tell me which meeting (10 or 100) would be less strenuous for your staff to pull together? The one for ten, right? How about getting the word out to get people there? Which would be more challenging. You say, "Stop right there. I don't know 10 of the right people to invite to such a dinner. I only know maybe one at best." To which I say, "And can you speak frankly to Jane to get her to bring the right number of her friends to the event?"

Can you imagine the subject for discussion that night? You don't need a big staff to know what the hot button topics are for your cause. Child welfare. Population health. There must be something that leaps out at you. Where to host the event? Maybe the donor's house or a restaurant, or some special setting. The three most important parts of the meal is: the list, the list, the list. Namely, the invitee list. These must be fresh names, ones with whom you're not that familiar. Know who they are before they get there, and take copious notes as the discussion ensues. And about that topic: make sure it circles back to your nonprofit seamlessly so as not to make it a blatant advertisement. But circle back certainly so people leave knowing you and your organization are the thought leaders on the subject.

As you listen to the conversation, transcribe it to have a lasting journal of the event. Without this, you will have lost a wonderful way to keep in touch with participants and get them to the next level of possibly supporting your cause. Can that journal be an article for the local newspaper or magazine in your field? If so, find a way to place it. You want that lasting impression.

You may find yourself licking envelopes to get out invitations to this meal. You're a small shop, you're used to that by now. Sure you may need to get your hands a little dirtier than the person working for the multinational nonprofit that can afford every resource under the sun. But you have partners in micromarketing that will make sure your hours don't become so long that you've given up a personal life.

The real challenge is not small staff but small plans. You have the ability to dream big, and you have the means to pursue greatness in addressing the needs of your beneficiaries and advancing you cause.

Go and be mighty!

# CHAPTER 17

## *Case Studies in Pitfalls*

We already covered one pitfall in a major gifts program. The last thing you want is for a donor to complain about you constantly trying to reach them. It is a hole out of which you may never climb. But what are some other landmines? Let's look at them by way of case studies.

*Thankful Grandmom.* A colleague told me this story. A woman's grandson was in a car accident and went to two hospitals. The first hospital, a general facility, treated the boy first as an emergency patient. Doctors stabilized him and moved him to a second hospital where staff worked till he recovered. She visited both afterward.

At the first hospital, grandmom walked into the emergency room. She expressed her intentions to show gratitude for their work by offering a gift. The nurse on duty chatted briefly with her, and concluded that there was a need for new microwave ovens throughout their department and in others. They got what they wished for: namely, five brand new microwave ovens. She then went to the second hospital. The nurse on duty there contacted the development office. They sat with the donor, and talked to determine what the best approach would be to help the hospital. Eventually, their conversations resulted in a $1 million donation. The difference between the two hospitals was that the second one had a more sophisticated system to receive donors. There was a culture of philanthropy so much that when somebody stopped by to discuss a gift, staff knew how to handle it.

Two lessons: promote a culture of philanthropy within your entire staff, but let your fundraisers handle conversations with donors. The professionals allow the discussion to flow gradually and purposefully so the needs of your cause and the donors' philanthropic goals are aligned. Professionals take a step back, know the story and tell it, and allow the donor to walk the garden path to the ultimate goal of expressing their gratitude by way of a gift.

*Alternate Endings.* Call this a tale of alternate endings. In the first story, a woman shows up at your nonprofit. She belongs to a church, and she says there's a member of the congregation who wants to give a gift of stock. She's talking to your receptionist. The receptionist talks to your controller, who is not very responsive. Your controller knows that money is money, however, and he talks to the woman and sends the appropriate paperwork to transfer the stock. That's the end of the story. As the fundraiser for the charity, you never hear anything about this. The gift of stock is never received.

In an alternate ending, the controller comes to you and tells you about this potential donation. He says he's got the paperwork and sends it to the donor. You tell him to give you the donor's contact information as well. You follow up about a week later to find that the donor is confused by the paperwork, and they have not forwarded it to their broker yet. You explain the paperwork, you guide them through the process, and you asked for the broker's phone number so you can continue the conversation. End result: the gift of stock arrives at your nonprofit about one month later.

The second ending is the one that happened to me. The stock was worth well into the six digits. If I hadn't been alerted to the situation, there was a very good chance we would have not received the gift. At this particular nonprofit, it was my job to facilitate such transactions. It was not the job of the controller or the receptionist or anybody else. The system worked. The previous ending was a story at another nonprofit where I worked. The information about the donor's contact was not kept, and I had no way of tracking the gift.

*Dropping a Gift.* Earlier in my major gift solicitation days, a consultant was coaching me. I had a handle on my portfolio of about a hundred major donors. He insisted that I drop off a special gift to their home. Simply walk up and drop the gift at their home. He said, "I have seen this done so well many times." At the time, I was apprehensive. Sure, I knew some of these donors, but none of them quite as well as to drop off something at their home. I followed my gut, and I did not walk up and drop off the gift. I did send a few of the donors a special gift via mail. In that the special gift raised awareness for our organization, it worked well.

Later in my work, I actually did find opportunities to drop off gifts. It was when I knew the donor well, and it was when I either was at their house previously or knew of a business address where I could drop it. It is a wonderful way to reinforce your message to that donor; you care about them and your cause is important for them to keep top of mind.

*Biggest Pitfall.* There is one fatal pitfall to avoid in major donor solicitation. Namely, it is lack of follow through. Use your calendar to remind you of follow through opportunities. Use the action items feature on your fundraising database to position your next steps. Whatever you do, don't leave follow through to chance. Certainly, as you probably already know, you won't necessarily get a callback. You need to be the one calling out to a major donor. Just make sure it's on the calendar – you don't want to be a nuisance and you don't want to lose an opportunity. There's a fine line between those two.

Nobody else is going to follow through on your major donor solicitations. Your successor won't necessarily come in and pick up where you left off. This is your portfolio to start, build, and work. As you work it, the biggest mistake you'll make is not moving donors to an ask.

# CHAPTER 18

## *Small Ways, Mighty Gratitude*

You've always heard it said, "Thank your donors." But for donors of very significant gifts, there is really only one primary thank you that will mean the most to them. There are others you can give along the way, however. Let's start with those.

If you work in a nonprofit, you know the importance of acknowledgments. You probably work with the team to get them out for your daily donations within a day or two. I've been militant about getting them out. When you're in the world of major gifts, you spend time thinking of little ways to send gratitude to your donors who are particularly generous. It may start with a personal note on there a particular thank you letter. But it begins to scale from there. Nothing about these special signs of gratitude are a big production.

I spoke about running a special gift to a donor prospect. It was a bottle of wine. How did I know he would like a bottle? Because we talked about it. When you talk with a major donor long enough, you get to learn more about their passions and interests. You can begin to get ideas of how to respond to their passions with the right thank you token. Would you spend this kind of time planning thank you notes for everyone on your list? You would if you had 18 hours to work each day. But for your smaller and esteemed portfolio, you can spend the time.

This is different from incentive gifts sent to donors in the mail. You know what I'm talking about. You've seen the dream catchers and the bookmarks. Those trinket gifts are a slippery slope when it comes to your entire mailing list. I've seen the data about how well they work, but to me they're only encouraging a need to upgrade the gift giving. But this is different. These are gifts that are much more personal.

Do you work in a children's program? Take a moment to have them draw a thank you as an art project on index cards. Or if you have the releases to do so, take a picture of them holding up a thank you sign they drew. Children have a wonderful way to help you make the donor feel special. Is there a graduation ceremony? Is there a talent show or other special event where the kids take center stage? Invite your major donors to be part of the festivities. Are you part of an arts organization? Give your major donors a chance to meet with the cast or the artists. There are ways to thank donors that you will only discover yourself because they are that unique to your cause and organization.

But the best gift of all mentioned at the beginning, what is that? It's not complicated. It goes beyond telling your donors what you used their funding for only last year. The greatest gift you can give them is telling them that their gift will leave a legacy for your nonprofit. In doing that, you will have shown them your gratitude in ways that will reap many more benefits. Being able to tell them this starts with a special, deliberate plan and fund for more significant gifts. It should be the reserves or endowment where you don't use the principal money in the account and keep it growing in forever. Tell them that their gift is being used for that scholarship or special recognition award or new ministry within your charitable work. Something that will last for years to come.

Imagine a donor has given you a substantial gift. You go back to them the following year and let them know that their gift is still funding ten scholarships each year to the most life-enriching program you offer. This is the reserve fund that is designated by the board to remain in effect and help for generations to come. You can show them over decades how many students will be assisting through their one gift. Do you think they will be more inclined to give you another gift?

How about when you consider another purpose that the fund may support in the future? The following year, when you expand the list of benefits of the reserve fund, you are laying the groundwork for an additional gift. It's much better than going back the following year and saying, "Thank you so much for that gift last year because it helped pay our electric bill for nearly an entire year." That doesn't have the same cache, right? Better to say, "With your funding, we established an account and we buy fresh produce for our pantry each and every year with the interest from that account. It is so helpful to give our families in need healthy food."

In my more than three decades working at charitable organizations, I've seen five- and six-digit gifts come in and go up like paper in fire through an operating fund. And it wasn't for lack of revenue, rest assured I was making my budgeted fundraising goals. It was because of the "found money" effect. It was like someone hit the lottery and went on a spending spree. And it's not like what they bought was bad. The extra expenditure could've been very necessary in fact, but just not budgeted. Now with found money, why not buy that thing or provide that service.

For some of these donors, this substantial gift represents money they earned over decades of work. It wasn't something they inherited, and it wasn't something that just landed in their laps. And it went up – like paper in fire. The money was spent on temporary help, on consulting contracts, on equipment...the spending was unplanned. These are not words you do you want affiliated with your nonprofit's budgeting process. More about that later.

What a wasted opportunity to steward a major gift and demonstrate to a donor how it will support your mission long term. Some of those gifts I'm speaking about were from estates of individuals who had no family. You might think, "They're not around anymore, and no kin, so no harm, no foul to use it right up." However, just because it came from one individual who is no longer around doesn't mean we couldn't have leveraged their gift to demonstrate to others how we grew a fund that keeps on giving forever.

How *does* the electric bill get paid? There needs to be an annual plan for that. Solicit more donors who are not major prospects and ask them if they can make a recurring gift. Save the five- and six-digit donors for what can last forever. It helps to get those prospects (not to mention the people of means they know who you may not know yet) thinking of other ways they can leave a legacy for your work.

Getting to the place where you can offer such a reserve or endowment fund will take time and energy on your part, but your donors won't be the only ones leaving a legacy. This will be your legacy as well.

## PART V
## *Feel Your Impact*

*"Courage is knowing what not to fear."*
      -    *Plato*

Where can you make an impact as a fundraiser? How about where angels fear to tread? Budgets, operations, spreadsheets… those places you don't necessarily want to go will only help you get the development office and entire organization to the right place. When you let others own your budget, you relinquish some control over your success. When you don't dig into some of the details regarding operations, you'll find yourself being asked to raise more money to cover shortfalls. Learn the spreadsheets, visit those dark corners of your operation, and learn how to make an impact where you never thought it could be felt.

## CHAPTER 19

### *Kapow! Make an Impact*

The whole section is about finance and budgeting, and I just didn't know how to give it more pizazz. So I took the most used word graphic that appeared on screen during the fight scenes in the 1960s classic television *Batman* series. You'll see how exciting finance and budgeting can be for a fundraiser once you read this section!

Go ahead and say it – I've heard it a hundred times from fellow fundraisers. "I'm not much of a numbers person," you say. It's understandable. You're in sales. You use language, either in written word or spoken, to move products or services. In this case, we call it fundraising. We can't all be good at everything, you say.

My response to that, "Get over it!"

There are two sides to sales, the actual selling and the tracking and analysis of sales. Maybe there was a day when you didn't need to know your numbers. That was a long time ago. Remember what the sharks teach: know your numbers cold. It's knowing the nitty gritty of your budget details that helps you succeed in this line of work. More accurately put, you can't trust others to know your work or numbers as well as you do.

The CFO helping you build your budget may know how to forecast but doesn't know everything. The controller taking your budget and spreading it through a 12-month calendar may know how to allocate but doesn't know everything. You are the one who knows the most about your business and how you raise money, and therefore your budget, allocations, and forecast – don't abdicate your responsibility to the finance team.

Isn't the word "abdicate" a little excessive? When you allow the CFO and controller to take your information at budget time and pass it through their own analysis and reporting, you have failed in your responsibility to take full ownership. Sure, let them float the numbers, but ultimately you are going to be the one who stands before the Board of Directors or executive team to explain what happened or didn't happen. And by then it may be too late to learn it all.

In the budget planning period, know your revenue goals as well as you know your expenses. You may have your expenses nailed down. Each mail piece, each stamp, copy/print services. And of course you do, those numbers are set to some extent. The price of a stamp is going up, you're sending out a certain number of pieces –and that is that. Forecasting is difficult, right? You better believe it is. That's why so many finance departments find it so difficult. The accounting team tries to do it well, but without your help they can't do it completely.

You know donations slack off in the summer, but do you know week by week when that starts to occur? Do you know the one-time larger gifts you've gotten during those times that may have bumped your numbers? Take away that four-digit gift you got in July, and look at the rest of the giving to make sure you're forecasting with reasonable numbers. You know that January and February are notoriously difficult moments to solicit gifts – but do you know the most cost-effective approach to reach out at the time? In short, know how to dig into data for answers you need.

After you know your data well, you sit with the finance team. Your CFO tells you what is reasonable to expect in revenue. Your controller may give you a three-year trend on revenue at your organization. However, you know that last year is the better indicator and the previous two years before that had many anomalies. This is experience talking. I have lived through freshman years where I didn't know the trends. I have lived through the finance team's projections, the ones that made me stutter during board meetings trying to explain shortfalls all year long. Sure, we made it to the end of the year just fine, but it was a struggle getting there.

Rewind a few months earlier. The finance team and I sat down briefly to discuss forecasts. They then put my data into their numbers crunching machine. We sit and review the results, but I didn't have much to say because I was new and didn't study the trends well enough. And at that time, I abdicated my responsibility. By the time I get to that board meeting months later, I was simply reaping what I'd sown.

There was a CEO at a consulting firm. To say he was colorful would be an understatement. He just had a way of saying things that has stayed with me for decades. If I was trying to explain to a client something in detail, and the end result was positive, he would say, "Give them the baby without the birthing pains!" He would say things like that. Sometimes I would look at him and say, "I'm not really sure what that even means."

But the one thing he said to me that stands out – the one thing that I often repeat mostly to myself but sometimes to a colleague is this. We were going through our annual audit, and of course there were many questions to be asked and answered. We were being asked about a process that was new to us, and frankly I think it was new to the auditors well. There was prodding and follow-up questions. Finally, this CEO said, "I'm not going to have some snot nose auditor telling me how to run my business!" I had never heard anybody speaking about an auditor that way. I must say, it was very enlightening.

His son also ran the business with him, and he was even more brazen. When the IRS reached out to one of our clients about a missed filing with penalties and fees and whatever adjustments needed to be made, I was ready to cave. The son said to me, "No, ask for forgiveness and tell them there was nothing you could do about it – get the penalty fees removed." To my surprise, the IRS did that.

These two were dynamite to work with, and I learned so much during my time with them. The most important thing I learned is: If I can lead auditors and the IRS to change their minds, I am not going to let some finance team run my forecasts or project my outcomes. Filmmaker Billy Wilder who once said, "Trust your own instinct. Your mistakes might as well be your own."

At the beginning of the budget process, you need to have your agenda set. Know how much your events are going to make, know how much your direct mail is going to bring in, be sure you have a handle on all of those revenue streams. That way, when the executive team or Board looks at you and ask how much more money you can generate to cover a shortfall, you can tell them, "This is the maximum. This is the budget." You have examined every possible option to raise revenue that you are aware of at this time. There is no magic, there is only the formula. As always, you want to under promise and over deliver, but never let them think you have some magic up your sleeve because they will want you to reveal it up front.

What if you really don't know spreadsheets? What if you're really bad at math? These are two very separate issues. Being bad at math can be resolved if you are good with spreadsheets. That may seem counterintuitive, but it really is not. Spreadsheets can do amazing things, but you don't need to know all of their capabilities. You just need to know simple things, like calculating or sorting. You are at a disadvantage if you don't embrace the spreadsheet because the people building them with your numbers can make mistakes. And those mistakes will ultimately fall back on you.

Mistakes on the spreadsheet can provide a false sense of security to a manager in another department. They think everything is going well, they don't watch out for certain costs because they feel they are under budget. The day comes when everyone learns that's not the case. All of a sudden, your expenses are much higher than you budgeted. Your revenue may be on budget, but you're in the red. If you're not careful, you can easily become the scapegoat.

What can you do to learn how to use spreadsheet software? Take a workshop. Watch a YouTube video. Play around with one on the weekends. The premise of the spreadsheet software is simple: put in numbers, and then you can do things with those numbers. With some formulas, you can make automatic calculations. With another button, you can sort data.

But even if you don't want to learn a spreadsheet software, familiarize yourself with some common mistakes. If numbers don't add up, formulas may not be working. It's simple: double check the math. Take a look at how your revenue projections have been allocated over 12 months. Does it look like the estimates work? Own it in the planning as well as you do in the execution.

There are so many workshops entitled, "Finance for the Non-financial Manager." There's a reason for this. People will do what their budgets allow them to do. If the numbers say they can spend, they will spend. And these are in areas that you have no control over. Areas like operations and HR. Areas like programs and sometimes marketing. The only problem with that is: You are the person who makes the money for them to spend.

Believe me, when the executives are reviewing a draft budget before they send it to the board, they will come to you if there is a loss being shown. They want a surplus, as they should in every case, and they may ask you to help create it. This is where having a set of projections well-rooted in realistic plans and expectations comes in very handy. "Can you add another event?" they will ask. Or they might ask, "Can't we just do another mailing?" You have to answer those questions for yourself, and do that well in advance of their inquiry. Do you already have enough events? Would you be able to handle one more? And how much would a new event make conceivably?

What happens if you are not invited to the budget discussions? Depending on your level of investment in the process, you need to push back on this. You should definitely be in that meeting. However, at the very least you need to document in detail how you reached your own conclusions. Document the final numbers you authorize. In the end, if you were still held responsible for numbers you did not create – it's time to consider if this is the right cause to spend your time.

If you started working with major donors, the executive team will invariably ask, "Can't we reach more of our supporters who can give us a more significant gift?" Be careful. This is a dangerous question to answer. Calling on donors of more significant means does not automatically mean you'll have a windfall.

# CHAPTER 20

## *An Obvious Nightmare*

My sister is a lawyer. Before one of her trials, she was telling me the fine points about the jury selection process. My advice to her, having zero experience except watching a lot of court dramas on television, "Select jury members who you think will side with your case." Her response? "Kind of obvious, but okay."

At the risk of you saying the same to me, I'll preface my next piece of enlightenment by saying, "It's not always obvious!" When it comes to significant gifts from major donors, always forecast conservatively. There, I said it. Certainly, you want to predict some level of success. But as in all giving, there is unpredictability. Competing charitable priorities for the donor, unstable conditions in the marketplace, maybe even unflattering news in the field in which you're operating – these are just a few things that could influence whether a gift comes in or not. Don't be forced to explain why revenue fell short of expectations. You want to manage those expectations instead.

Major gifts have a tendency to throw off your budget planning as much as they can throw off your operating fund. Imagine a five- or six-digit gift unexpectedly shows up in the mail. Better still, what if it walked in the front door! This is what happened at a human services charity where I worked. This man walked in the door. His appearance was tattered. The receptionist recalled how she was prepared to hand this senior wearing a ripped jacket and dirty sneakers a referral sheet so he could find services.

To her surprise he reached into his pocket and pulled out a check for a gift worth nearly six-digits. He was a retired priest, and that money was all he had left to give. The church would take care of him the rest of his life, so he was able to give this generously. We went into gratitude mode, thanking him and wanting to get his background story a little. There was no need to pursue him any further, this would be his last major gift to this or any charity.

What did we do with his gift? Used it up in that year's operating account. And again not because we didn't meet our budgeted goals for revenue. We just spent more that year. And it's not like what we spent money on wasn't to help others—this donor would be happy to know his funding helped somebody. But if you have a plan to use major gifts to help people in a legacy endowment, you have a better probability of getting more of those substantial donations.

Consider this. If you don't separate those major donations from the rest, you could be held by that standard next year. Why did we make so much in this quarter last year but didn't repeat that performance this year? That's because you had one or two really significant gifts included with all the rest. Your major gift budget needs to be listed as a separate line item if at all possible.

I worked for one ministry where I spent some time with the outgoing director. We had an interesting conversation about estate gifts. He said to me, "It's great to work here – because you have your budget but with one big estate gift you could make that within your first six months of the year." He wasn't a bad director. He thought he just knew the rules of the game. You can't budget for major gifts, but you can sure enough reap the benefits when they arrive.

The only problem is: what if they don't arrive? One of the first things I did at that ministry was to put major gifts and donations in average ranges in their own separate line items. It was less confusing to run two separate line items and plan for each.

Similarly, online giving can throw you off if you're not planning properly. Online gifts are on the increase, and this is especially true when you take into account peer-to-peer fundraising. This is where instead of getting one gift at your website, multiple gifts are given because a person sends their plea for help on your behalf to their "peers" through social media. Unless you're a major international charity with millions of followers, this strategy may not flow as virally as you would like. Still, it works. It's important for you to know how well it works, in fact.

Digging into online giving and all data is important when it comes to planning your budget. You had a fantastic month in January. Donations may have been flat in direct mail, but online giving saved the day! Isn't that wonderful! Until you dig into the data to find out that one of your donors who traditionally mails a four-digit gift sent it instead this year as a response to a friend who posted a plea on social media. The good news: if direct mail sales are flat and online gained ground by cannibalized direct mail sales, at least you still have some growth there. But don't start planning for online gifts to go through the roof in January.

The longer you dig through the data, the better your budgeting process. Getting at the raw data is not as tricky as it sounds, but yes it is as tedious as it sounds. Who has time for all that? Maybe you don't, but maybe a person volunteering with you currently has some experience. With the right spreadsheet, you could more easily analyze these numbers. "There he goes ranting about the power of the spreadsheet again," you might say. The better your forecasts, the better your monthly actuals will look in comparison. This will make your executive team (dare I say it) happy as well as your Board of Directors.

Somebody once told me budgeting for major gifts is like using a stopwatch to predict lightning. That person didn't do a whole lot in the way of outreach to major donors in a serious, disciplined way. When it comes to major gifts, sure sometimes lightning strikes, but hopefully with enough consistency in your relationship building, you can become the lightning rod.

What is said of the most important personal relationships in your life can also be said of developing better business relationships with major donors: you get what you give. If you don't spend enough time with your children growing up, you can expect them to not spend a whole lot of time with you as you get older. If you're not sure what I mean, grab a box of tissues and go listen to Harry Chapin's song "Cat's in the Cradle."

Budget time with your major donors, then you can begin budgeting for the kinds of investments you hope they can make.

# CHAPTER 21

## *Smooth Operator*

Fundraisers should know their revenue and expenses inside and out, but what about all the other costs at your charitable organization? What influence can you exert to contain those expenses? Isn't that the job of the chief operating officer? What does a fundraiser know about operations anyway? And if you did try to have a say in this area, will you simply be shut down – as in the executive team saying, "That's really none of your business. All you need to do is raise money."

On some counts, the team may be right. Certainly, you wouldn't want another area getting into your day-to-day operations to help you find best fundraising practices. The phrase is, "Stay in your lane." However, there are ways to stay in your lane and still have an impact on cost containment.

An executive team member looked at me toward the end of one fiscal year to say, "Everything would've been OK, but we didn't make enough revenue." I examined the spreadsheets to determine that we made the amount of fundraising money budgeted. And if we were off a single digit percentage point or two, it is the responsibility of the entire team to figure out how to match that with reduced expenses and stay in line. My experience has shown that if you are meeting your budget expectations for revenue, your board treasurer will acknowledge that. So where was that budget shortfall to which that person was referring? In this case, it was in other revenue, government program reimbursement revenue, which was not under the fundraising department. I was able to drill down with the team to make sure everyone knew where the shortfall existed.

No matter if your revenue is on target or if either revenue falls short or expenses are out of control, there is a problem. If you have an overextended line of credit, second and third mortgage on your facility, or (the worst) failure to meet payroll, what does it matter if you hit your own fundraising goals? This is not a call to get into everybody's business. This is simply a call to take ownership with other leaders of the organization. Let's talk about ownership.

There are five levels of worker for any business but especially nonprofit. Where do you fit in these five levels? Sure, some of it is driven by your job title, but not all of it. You will see that the five levels are somewhat interactive, and it may be difficult to see how you fit in. But you're here somewhere.

The first level is the front line staff, better known as worker bees. They execute on plans from above. They get the work done that moves your organization along. They are indispensable, except when they're not doing their jobs. It is one of the most gut-wrenching tasks of all, determining whether a person can stay with the team or needs to be terminated. If a person is not working out and you've given them a few chances, it's only for the best of the organization that you part company. That is never easy, and this is not an HR book. And let's assume that the person is working out very well and getting things done! With any luck and if there's an opening, they move up.

The next level of work or a supervisor. One of the more thankless jobs admittedly. Let's face it, you are neither full management nor the front line worker bee. You are somewhere in between. You have to hear all the griping from the front line, and you have to take all the plans (and sometimes posturing) of the brass. Yet somehow through it all you're supposed to increase goals and meet expectations. And let's say you do the right thing: motivate your team, understand your goals, streamline your processes, and ultimately make improvements all the way around. You may make it to the next level.

The next level as managerial director. Well, haven't you arrived! You are considered a subject matter expert, and now you're on the task of managing more people or processes or both. Either way, the expectations are even higher as are the stakes. You must now move an entire division forward having even more influence on whether the nonprofit succeeds.

The next level is executive. They spent most of their time in the strategizing. Or at least they should have. Some do, some don't. Some executives stay on the managerial level because it's comfortable there, but they will learn quickly that is not acceptable. In the C-Suite, they really do need to be thinking strategically. Something that's easy to say but difficult to do. It means having a compelling vision, explaining it, and advancing it to not only staff but the Board. And while you're at it, you need to connect to your vision so that your donors and community understands and accepts it as well. The thoughts you're thinking, the plans you're making, will have an impact on the entire organization, field, and community, especially if you're doing your job well. This is not an easy or enviable task.

The next level is ownership. That's the highest level, yet it should be shared by everyone. If you have it, you know it. If you don't, you need to get it. The supervisor, the worker bee, the manager—everyone is an owner. Which gets back to my original premise: you have to take ownership even in the areas of budgeting and operations.

One of my first jobs out of college was the manager of a bookstore. The owner was a driver no doubt. This was at a time when online retailers were not an issue – but the big bookstore chains were just starting up, and she was starting to feel the heat. Recognizing that there is an entire generation that hasn't even stepped foot into a bookstore, I guess this all shows my age a little bit.

Being fresh out of college, I wasn't ready for a managerial job. But the real problem? I wasn't ready to own it. She specifically told me to take more ownership. "And this just doesn't mean the big stuff," she said to me. "You need to watch the little stuff. If there's a candy wrapper on the floor, you pick it up yourself. Nobody else will come along and pick it up if you don't."

My brother had another way of putting it. While I was still in high school, I worked at a convenience store. When I was first starting he said to me, "You need to take the initiative." I didn't know what that meant. So I asked him. And he said, "Start with something simple like taking the trash out. If you see the trash is filled, take it out. No one is going to argue with you for taking the trash out." He was right. And taking the initiative took me very far in my career.

One of the strongest influences in my life was my father. What did he tell me? "Find the job that nobody else wants to do," he said, "and do it." I guess you could relate this to taking out the trash, but he had something bigger in mind. "Like taking minutes at a meeting – nobody wants to do that. So do it. You don't have to be the best at doing it, because nobody else was doing it anyway. Just do it." And yes he said this to me long before Nike started using this as their slogan. Well, am I still dating myself now? Is that slogan still being used?

Take the initiative and get involved. Back to my one story mentioned in Chapter 5 about a client who was cashing in their CDs to catch up with shortfalls in their budget. Like most times, you can study a spreadsheet and find out where the money is leaking. In the case of this client, their problem was an international agreement that left them paying out way more than they ever took in. Nobody wanted to address the issue. We discovered it as their consulting team and brought it to their attention. The board said, "It's an agreement, what can we do?" It was our job to guide them through what would ultimately become the terribly difficult work to change the policy and stop the money drain. The organization exists today, which is not where it was heading. But it started because we as the development team took ownership and spoke up.

Getting back to exerting influence over operations, how do you "just do it." It's not simple, but there are areas of your fundraising division that influence other parts of the business. Let's take a simple one: volunteering. Perhaps you are in charge of volunteers, maybe you're not. But if people are donating anything to your organization, you should have oversight of that area. Volunteerism is donating time. I could get into how corporate volunteers will help you access corporate funding – so it should definitely be in your department.

What can volunteers do these days? If they're doing anything for you now, it's probably pretty simple. Maybe they are helping to serve meals or walking dogs at the shelter or ushering at an arts event. If you're a community-based group, this may be the proving ground for new volunteers who will ultimately be nominated to the Board of Directors.

However, volunteers can do so much more. They can do professional level work, so long as it doesn't involve the handling of money on a corporate level (certainly they can take tickets and make change at the registration or merchandise table). That said, perhaps there are some jobs around your nonprofit that could be just as well handled by volunteers instead of hiring. This speaks to the one budget item that costs the most for organizations: payroll.

All this to say that volunteerism is one area where you can exert your influence at reducing costs. At one facility where I worked, one that had a warehouse, volunteers gave thousands of hours each year – saving us enough personnel time equal to 10 full-time workers. While I was there, we worked hard to get volunteers from the warehouse to do other things. Where else could they serve? How else could they help? And in some cases, it saved us staff time. This caring group of people can help you operate more efficiently.

Other expense areas that may be under your control are marketing and public relations and of course all your fundraising costs. Certainly, to be in command of all these expenses is mandatory. Unfortunately, they don't make up the bulk of your expenses. You must find ways to get out some of the larger expenses. Staffing happens to be one of those expenses. If there are exorbitant staff expenses, it's probably not with your staff. It is probably the operating staff overall. For you to address that will require diplomacy for certain, but that's why you were hired for this job.

No, you are not the one to take the reins of operations, I'm not saying that at all. But you can exert some influence, and you must if you want to take ownership and see the organization thrive.

# CHAPTER 22

## *Leading Board Leadership*

An acquaintance from a long time ago called out of the blue one day. His request: "I started a new nonprofit, and I was hoping with your background in nonprofit you could be on the board." That one sentence had so many things wrong with it, and I can't begin to tell you what was going through my mind. I told him to start by telling me what the nonprofit was about. It was a sensitive subject. Suffice it to say his life had been touched by tragedy and he want to start a group to make sure that awareness was raised about the cause of that tragic event.

My first reaction was to tell him that there were other charitable groups doing this kind of work. He insisted that there weren't any doing this work the way he was going to do it. The nonprofit industry is splintered with far too many organizations and some of them trying to do the same exact thing as another. I told him if he wanted to start a nonprofit, he would have to work it for a couple of years before he could get officially recognized by the IRS. Perhaps what he was talking about was becoming a foundation or taking some donations he had already received and start a fund with the community foundation. Either way, it was going to take a lot of work.

Then I leveled with him. I told him that the Board of Directors has a very important responsibility. It needs to be the fiduciary agent for a nonprofit cause. It needs to demand that a surplus budget is forecast, not to mention realized, each and every year. Otherwise, the organization goes under. More importantly, it needs to raise money. Each and every board member needs to participate in doing that. They may not all know millionaires, and certainly they may not be wealthy themselves, but they can all do something to bring in revenue.

A couple decades ago now, I ran several boards of directors for nonprofit clients as a consultant. I was managing three or four boards at one time. This was a diverse group of health organizations, medical societies, nurses groups and physician associations. My brother put it best when he admitted that he didn't know exactly what I did for a living and told people, "He just runs things." I'm not sure but I think he made it sound like I worked for the mob.

During this time working with all these different boards, I came to a lot of realizations. First, there was a lot of reasons that people wanted to help lead an organization. Maybe it was to put the experience on their resume to advance their career, maybe it was for the prestige to be working alongside their peers, or maybe they wanted personal fulfillment. In some cases, it's because they wanted to do good. Whatever the reason, it usually wasn't too assume fiduciary responsibility for an organization that would legally bind them should something go dreadfully wrong.

What I saw among many boards of directors in my lifetime it's a lack of understanding of just how important that fiscal duty is. I've also seen times when a board will take matters into their own hands and be very involved. But many board members are complacent enough to allow the executive staff run the show—that is, until the expenses climb higher than the revenue. Then things can start to get ugly in the board room.

If it is the board's responsibility to raise money, then it is your responsibility to help them get there. How many times do you meet with your board members individually, over a cup of coffee? When was the last time you asked them what kind of contacts they have made in the world that they can bring to your cause? Or is there an event they attend that you should be attending as well. Or can they participate in another event because there are so many on the calendar and you're unable to get to them all. Your board should be receiving emails from you regularly inviting them to participate in some community event or your own event or just to introduce you to somebody.

And what of your board make up? When you start meeting with major donors, can you suggest somebody that would be good for your board? Certainly, your executive team will make those suggestions as well. And for sure, your nomination committee of volunteer leaders should be selecting an otherwise vetting people for committees and the board.

As you find major donors out in the world, do you run these names by the board to see who knows who? You can't be connected to everybody, you need to find warm introductions along the way from your volunteer leaders. Do you take advantage of their connections?

Does your executive team allow you access to the board? If they don't, that's a major problem. You always have some access to board members, either through a committee or by other interactions. How did your executive team act when you are speaking in front of the board? Remember that executive staff is the direct report for these volunteer leaders, and they will look to that team for overall leadership of the organization. Sometimes that executive team will insulate itself with the board for self-preservation. You can easily be on the outside looking in for cases like that. However, as you come to the board with new ideas and how to get more from them in the area of fundraising, your executive team should become more open to it. I have not seen an executive team yet who doesn't appreciate somebody taking the initiative to speak with board members one-on-one over coffee.

More often than not, today's board wants big results. They want to know that your team is working on getting major donors to take an interest in your cause. Your executive is the gate keeper, but you are the expert. You need to exert this kind of influence and take charge of your area. That will win the confidence of your executive and the entire board. In nonprofit, this is no time to be timid.

In the past few chapters, we have covered the ways in which you can influence the work of your nonprofit outside of the fundraising area. You can help build budgets, you can help keep operating costs down, and you can work with your board leadership in meaningful ways. In all these areas you have more than a passing influence.

# PART VI

## Revolution and Evolution

*"Everything will be okay in the end, and if it's not okay it's not yet the end."*

*-John Lennon*

You've got to start your nonprofit's finance revolution somewhere. Focus on a surplus operating account, meantime build your major gifts program to feed the other two funds. Where will you start? You don't need a perfect plan, you only need a good first step. Before you know you it, you and your team will be visiting donors for coffee and hosting dinners. Will you launch flawlessly? No. Will you work diligently? Yes. Will you be successful? If you follow through and keep at it, certainly.

Regarding the final chapter, it seems odd to get through a whole book then have a chapter called "Conclusion." The word may give an impression of summary or regurgitation of earlier points. Books should be transformative... and the last chapter should encourage you to evolve, to take what your learned and inspire you to go forth and do good! Thus the name here. In this last chapter of the book, don't look for a reiteration. Far from it.

# CHAPTER 23

## *First Steps*

We covered the three funds, nonprofit structure, our role as fundraisers, the importance of major gifts, the parts of a nonprofit you didn't know you can influence, and it all comes down to this—finding your starting point. Nonprofits come in all shapes and sizes. Some have facilities and some don't. Some get reimbursed from the government for services and some don't. Some have a large base of support and some don't. I don't know where you are. But if you are looking for a place to start, here are some suggestions.

The first step might be a step back to ask some questions. Have you ever thought about working with donors who can make a more significant contribution to your cause? Listen, not all nonprofits do. Some get their reimbursement from government fee-for-service. They exist on that for many years, until reimbursement starts to dry up and now they start wanting to cultivate a culture of philanthropy.

Do you know your donors? Do you want to get to know them better? I would suspect that if you picked up this book, you are at least curious about the possibility of beginning a major gifts program. Before you ask anything else, "Who are our major donors?" Or "How are we going to approach them?" Or even "Should we host a gala?" Ask this first: "What is going to be our major gift acceptance policy?"

Is this any different from the budget you keep for your life? You get a nice refund check from the IRS or maybe a holiday bonus from work. What's the first question you ask? How much of this am I going to spend? How much can I spend? How much am I going to save? Or what bill am I going to pay off? In other words, you need to figure out how much you're going to save for a rainy day and how much you're going to spend on that hot new kitchen product you want or new car you've been needing or a day at the spa. You have a budget in your mind.

If a gift is under a certain amount, it may all go right into the operating account. This would only be right. Look, not every gift gets saved for a rainy day. A kid gets a buck, he's not saving it for a rainy day, he's buying a candy bar. If he gets twenty dollars, well now he might save a little for a rainy day. If a mid-level gift comes in, decide how much you'll want to use now and how much gets put aside. If a real whopper of a gift comes in, now may be the time you put most of that away for a rainy day. Depending on how big the gift, you may want to open that endowment fund. Of course, all of this is best planned out in the budgeting phase.

Are you starting your major gifts program to cover a deficit or multiple years of deficit spending? Hold up. Maybe you should rethink that. Get your budget in line now by reining expenses against the revenue that's already coming in. The best start to a major gift plan is surplus budgeting with the normal gifts you receive now. Major gifts are poor performers under pressure. Besides, the more your revenue increases in deficit spending, the more your deficit will grow despite your efforts.

Now that you know what you're going to do with the gifts when you get them, how do you approach these donors? Do you know your top donors? You know the ones who give the most money – but how do you find the ones able to give a larger gift? These are the ones you want to spend time getting to know. If it's just you working on this project, give yourself a realistic goal. Tell yourself you can only reach out to 25 top donors in a given year. How do you find those donors? You could just go by the number of gifts you receive from your supporters now, and the size of the gifts they're giving. You know somebody is consistently giving you $5,000 each year, they are able to be generous. But not all of them will give like that.

Do yourself a big favor. Take your most recent donors, and the ones that give you more rather than less. Put the names in an Excel spreadsheet and run them through a wealth screening tool. Find your local library or some other place that has the wealth screening tool. It could be a local United Way or some other resource. You don't want to buy the screening source if you don't have to. The funny thing about data is that you have to know what you're going to do with it. Gathering it should be less challenging, working it is a whole other proposition. There is many a development office that gets some wealth data and does nothing with it. Or more times than not the fundraiser starts making calls to major donors but doesn't follow through just because donors don't seem interested. The fact is: you're not on their radar. They won't call you back from just one call, it may take several attempts.

This is tedious work because it is essentially niche marketing, and it is first a discipline. Is there an element of art to it? Yes, but it is science first. The art presents itself, normally at the end of cycles of hard work and precision labor. People who enter marketing with thoughts of the artistic process are really interested in advertising and design. Marketing (like major donor solicitation) is more of a business than that.

And for nonprofits, it's the right business to be in. The tax reform of recent years raised the standardized deduction for everyone. I thought about this as my peers concerned themselves with how lower level gifts could conceivably decline. My hopes were in larger gifts becoming more prevalent. It only seemed natural that larger gifts would increase as people had to meet a higher threshold for achieving a deduction.

Turns out that's exactly what happened. In the first year of the new higher standard deduction, the number of larger gifts (ones valued at more than $1,000) increased by 2.6% while the number of smaller gifts decreased by 4.4%. The number of donors for smaller gifts declined as well. It would be a good time to pursuing larger gifts through niche marketing.

Take that info to your board and executive leadership. Tell them it's time to get started on you major gifts program – and you have the blueprint to do it!

## CHAPTER 24

## *The Word Unspoken*

When you use words very casually, some become trivial catchphrases or worse cliché. We can begin ignoring them if we're not careful. They become muted in our minds. One example may include (ironically), "Actions speak louder than words." There are other ways to say this, and it would benefit all of us to consider that other phraseology because we get desensitized to clichés like this. The sentiment is still an important one, namely that we show more by what we do than what we say.

Or how about one of my favorites, "Don't judge a book by its cover." This one is borderline ridiculous. We judge books by their covers all the time, don't we? For some of you, you see a romance novel cover and immediately want to read it (or run from it). Or how about this book? Some have picked it up and said, "Too business-like, looks boring!" But should we judge people in this way? Underlying this cliché is a very true maxim: get to know somebody before placing a value judgment on them.

In this day of marketing and targeted messaging in the world of nonprofit, there are many words we use to make a point. Then they become overused. The one that's overused the most is the one not used in this book until now. That word is: sustainability.

Consider the word much like the phrase, "It's all about relationships," a phrase very much overused when it comes to major donor solicitation. The word "sustainability" is crucial to our work plans and thoroughly overworked. That fact doesn't make the word any less important. Because we are all about setting up the three funds—annual, reserve, and endowment—to keep us doing good work moving forward and protecting it for years to come.

Sustainability. Everybody talks about it, but who's doing anything about it. At least you can do a little to "build relationships" for any of your funds, so it's not just lip service. But sustainability, heck you have to work at that, and for funds you won't be able to access so freely. Maybe you throw around the word with no idea of its weight. Well, this is your chance to stop talking about it and start working it.

You need your board involved for sure. Your executive team, certainly. But first you have to say to yourself: "Charity begins at home in your heart." You have to believe that sustainability isn't just a word to say. It's a commitment—the way you work, the profession you've chosen.

# CHAPTER 25

## *Evolution: Everyone Leaves a Legacy*

Does everyone evolve? Not really. Some people evolve and others want to keep things the same. They cling to old ways, never wanting to try anything new. Similarly, some people have a legacy that lives on forever. Others don't seem to leave much that lives on. I'd say everyone leaves something in the great path of life. For some it's a morsel, for others it's a legacy. And I don't mean being so wealthy that they name stuff after you. Who wants that anyway?

Let's say they named some roadway after me, like the "Admiral Sims Boulevard." Not sure where the "admiral" came from but let's roll with it. Where does that get you? You'll just have people saying, "Oh, don't take that Admiral Sims Boulevard to get into town. What a nightmare! It's always crowded, and the potholes!" Or how about having a building named after you. The Sims Dormitory. "Dude that was an awesome party at the Sims last night!" I can see why people want to have stuff named after them, but the real legacy is in the change that is affected and the good that continues for centuries to come.

We live forever through our energy and our memories and our families or friends or communities. It's the generations or the positive influences you've left behind. Part of what makes us whole can be found in generations that came before, and you'll leave your mark on branches of the family tree yet to blossom or roads in the town yet to be paved, whether they're named after you or not. It all depends on how you invest your time, your energy, your love, and yes your money.

Jordan was a machinist. He never made much money, but he never had any kids either. The result: his money didn't fly out the window like it does when you have kids. Come on let's face it! My two daughters are lovely, but raising kids takes money, and it takes a good bit of yours. So Jordan leaves a six-digit gift to a local school. What if the school received that gift and it went up in the same fiscal year? End of story I suppose… Or what if it was placed in an endowment and offered the interest for decades to come. Then that guy's nieces and nephews and their children can keep advising on how the fund is to be used. It could inspire them to give in the future as well.

What you do, what you plan to do with people's gifts says more about you than your institution trying to help people day in and day out. People are like institutions. Or should I say institutions are like us. They are born, they struggle through early years, they mature and become wise, and (if they are truly wise) they leave behind a family of legacy builders who keep the good will going. This is about way more than money, it's about progress of the good. It's about advancing what's right and just.

But it's not only for the good.

Don't think for a second hate isn't advanced along with good. Oh the good and the bad live together here, and the hate can find a legacy just as the good can. Racism, crime, anger. Families can spend their generations promoting ugly causes just as they can promoting good ones.

A few years ago, I worked for a religious order of nuns. They were the kindest, most thoughtful, and most forward-thinking group I ever served. The one thing that seems prevalent in most of these groups is that members of their club are aging out. If you've seen an order like this you know what I mean. It's often called "the graying of the order." It's no secret that fewer young people are willing to make the sacrifice necessary to join these orders.

As stories about the "graying" have been passed around, there was one about an order of priests that was beyond gray. They were gone. They had all died. Yet because of sound financial planning—embracing the three funds—their work continues as strong as ever. Interest from an endowment helps fund programs, and secular staff still raise funds for annual operations. Their funds, their legacy, their giving spirit outlived their brotherhood.

Is being in nonprofit a calling? Is this a job? Is it a little of both?

One Sunday, I found myself thinking about an event that goes on year after year for a community film festival (a past employer). The Sunday was Oscar night. Years before, the festival leadership did not want to continue hosting the party. In fact, one year they skipped it. When I started there, current leadership worked with me to study the challenges of the party and bring it back. First, we ended the party when the Oscars began, so it became sort of a pre-party. Secondly, we brought the cost down to host a party at a much reduced ticket price. We made changes like that. I don't attend that event anymore – and haven't for years. Yet it continues.

Why does this event continue? You could say it's because it raises money every year, but it doesn't raise that much. You could say it's because the Oscars happen every year, and they are compelled to host this party. But that wasn't the case always in the past. No, it's because there was enough energy built around cultivating new leadership to continue the work of the organization. My primary role (as my job was appointed by and funded by a modest arts grant from the state) was to bring people to the leadership table who could carry on the work of this particular festival and that event. That's the way you build a legacy and work that carries on. Incidentally, the group had decided to fold, such is the challenge of trying to find new leadership. However, a few of us will pick up the pieces and try to host a new event with a fresh perspective. The same happened to a music festival in town. One event fell away but another one came to take its place. It seems there are lifecycles.

My father was a carpenter. He loved to build things, like houses, malls, a home for my mom and us kids. He helped to revitalize downtown Philadelphia with a mall that revolutionized urban development at the time. It's probably one of the reasons I love the Center City section of the town today. That mall fell into disrepair. Eventually, the structure he built was empty, abandoned.

Now it's being revitalized again. A facelift, new shops, people are coming back. The bones he and the workforce put together had lasting value. He would be proud to see it come back to life. If he were around, I can hear him say, "You can't keep a good structure down for long." It's a shame he's not around to see it.

When I was little, as he was driving around Philadelphia, he'd point out houses and whole neighborhoods of houses he'd helped to build. These weren't big mansions, in fact quite the opposite. He said doing his job was his way of helping people. His saying that probably led me to a life in nonprofit work, but he never urged me to do one line of work over another. He was always good about letting us kids find our own path. "You're smart," he'd say. "You'll figure it out." And we all did. And I feel like now I'm building as well, not houses like he did but building up programs and good works that others do in the world. He was an inspiration, and that was his legacy.

My dad died a few years back, but is he not around? He had five children, and we certainly share his perspective and demeanor? Didn't my eyes come from him, as well as my upbringing, the parts of me that appreciate the emotion of a rebirth or an underdog story? Because my dad didn't just build a mall or a house, he left part of himself in each door frame or rooftop, and most importantly among his children and grandchildren. He built a family legacy. We represent branches with solid roots on which to grow. Our leaves may fall, but each spring comes the promise of new life. In fact, each season brings something different. This tree didn't grow mighty and strong in one season but over many decades and centuries.

Charity begins at home, but where it goes from there depends on all of us. All of us mothers. All of us fathers. And sisters. And brothers. Sons and daughters. Our goal as fundraisers needs to be about making this year's budget, but it should be building a legacy. Are you going to leave your mark or will you leave a morsel?

THE END

www.ingramcontent.com/pod-product-compliance
Lightning Source LLC
Chambersburg PA
CBHW032005190326
41520CB00007B/359